W9-BZE-700

ISBN 00 0 110492 9

Fakers

9a∆
MAL

Fakers

*Hoaxers, Con Artists, Counterfeiters,
and Other Great Pretenders*

Paul Maliszewski

JOHNSTON PUBLIC LIBRARY WITHDRAWN
JOHNSTON IA 50131

THE NEW PRESS

NEW YORK
LONDON

Parts of this book appeared, in different form, in *The Baffler, Bookforum, In These Times, McSweeney's,* the *Philadelphia Independent,* and *Wilson Quarterly* as well as on the Web site Moby Lives. Thanks be to the editors at those publications. Thanks also to Monique Dufour, Steve Featherstone, and Jim McNeill, who read and commented on early drafts. Special thanks to Sarah Fan, my editor at The New Press, who first encouraged me, back in the spring of 2000, to keep writing about fakes. Sarah is an editor without parallel: patient, insightful, and true.

© 2008 by Paul Maliszewski
All rights reserved.
No part of this book may be reproduced, in any form,
without written permission from the publisher.

Requests for permission to reproduce selections
from this book should be mailed to:
Permissions Department, The New Press,
38 Greene Street, New York, NY 10013.

Published in the United States by The New Press, New York, 2009
Distributed by W. W. Norton & Company, Inc., New York

LIBRARY OF CONGRESS CATALOGING-IN-PUBLICATION DATA

Maliszewski, Paul.
Fakers : hoaxers, con artists, counterfeiters, and other great pretenders
/ Paul Maliszewski.
    p.   cm.
ISBN 978-1-59558-422-9 (hc)
1. Imposters and imposture—Biography.   I. Title.
CT9980.M155   2009
813'.4—dc22   2008028362

The New Press was established in 1990 as a not-for-profit alternative to the large, commercial publishing houses currently dominating the book publishing industry. The New Press operates in the public interest rather than for private gain, and is committed to publishing, in innovative ways, works of educational, cultural, and community value that are often deemed insufficiently profitable.

www.thenewpress.com

Composition by dix!
This book was set in Adobe Caslon

Printed in the United States of America

2   4   6   8   10   9   7   5   3   1

To Hadley

Verisimilitude is, by my lights, a technique one exploits in order to assure the reader of the truthfulness of what he's being told. If he truly believes he is standing on a rug you can pull it out from under him. Of course verisimilitude is also a lie.

—John Cheever,
interview with the *Paris Review*, 1976

CONTENTS

I, Faker

I must confess now. I must tell what I have done.

I was a staff writer at a business newspaper. When called upon, I was an editor of sections on annuities, executive gift giving, and year-end wrap-ups. I was a hack and I knew it. What's more, I had come to see my hackwork as not just flimsy and inconsequential but damaging. I continued to pump out article after article, however, covering businesses in central and upstate New York for our readers, the business owners of central and upstate New York. One of my stories, about a welfare-to-work program that was 100 percent free of interviews with any actual workers, received praise from the publisher for being balanced. Like Lake Onondaga, located just miles from where I wrote, my articles not only smelled a little peculiar, they polluted the air around me. They were toxic.

Perhaps I could have tolerated being employed as a poorly paid hack for many more years, but once having seen my hackwork as dangerously simplistic, I could not again look away. I needed to write a letter to the editor, addressing all the issues the paper consistently ignored. Why hadn't we written a single article about Bennett Funding Group, Inc., the Syracuse-based company at the center of the largest Ponzi scheme in history? Bennett's paper empire took in more than twelve thousand investors from forty-six states to the tune of $1.5 billion, and the bankruptcy proceedings unfolded only an hour's drive from our newspaper's office. Why was one of my colleagues writing an editorial about the NAACP, placing at the crux of his sterling analysis the marital history of its current president? While Syracuse burned, the publisher acted as if the civility of the nation depended on the distinction between "who" and "whom," the managing editor practiced calling himself with a cellular phone he received compliments of an advertiser, for research purposes, and the other writers battled over "among" and "amongst."

"Invest Aggressively in OSHA Penalties to Enhance Corporate Profits," *Business Journal of Central New York*, September 1, 1997

To the Editor:

Three cheers and then some for Norm Poltenson's "Ladder without Rungs" editorial in the August 4 issue of the *Business Journal*. Poltenson points out that the United States, with its dynamic, revolutionary economy, is by far the superior of Europe, but he misses the opportunity to capitalize on an important fact: American CEOs are also more successful than their European counterparts. I should say *tremendously* more successful. In the United Kingdom, for instance, the ratio of what a typical worker is paid to what a CEO is compensated is a paltry 1:33. In Germany, CEOs get a laughable 21 times what the common worker *volk* takes home. In the United States, meanwhile, the ratio of what a typical worker receives to what a CEO takes home is 1:120. Also, the richest 0.5 percent of our population (many of them our CEOs, thank you very much) owns 31 percent of the stock in this country. The same cannot be said for the countries of Europe, whose own stock markets have been seen flat on their backs, overcome by weak knees and blurry vision at the mere sight of our triumphant Dow.

However, earlier this week my American reverie was shattered as I read that the ungrateful workers at UPS have gone on strike. The men (and women) in brown are saying the company hired too many part-time workers and that they are required to lift loads that are too heavy and handle too many packages an hour. Please, I thought. First brush aside these sugary, humanist sentiments, and let's get down to facts. UPS carriers are required to lift packages weighing up to 150 pounds. Sorters are expected to handle 1,600 packages per hour. While I'm not sure I can lift 150 pounds or even count to 1,600 in an hour, the brown people of UPS are, in fact, professional sorters and carriers and naturally suited for this kind of work. It is their job to sort and carry. Moreover, they should cease with their shrill complaints. If the striking brown clowns (workers) should dare seek a more humane corporation, they would do better to seek a good psychotherapist.

To put the complaints of those UPSers in perspective, let's consider the true success of the company. In 1996, UPS made $1 billion in profits. But it hasn't been all up. Since 1990, UPS has paid $4.4 million in penalties for health and safety complaints, for more than 1,300 violations documented by the Occupational Safety and Health Administration. Let us assume, conservatively, that those violations and penalty payments were made in equal amounts over the last seven years. Thus, UPS paid about $630,000 for an average of 186 violations a year. I bring this up not to berate UPS, as the *New York Times* did. Rather, I want to suggest that the penalty (a trifle really for a billion-dollar corporation) is in effect one of the wisest investments it could make. Indeed, in order to continue on its path to success and improve its already considerable profit margins, UPS must act aggressively now and take risks. One way to do this is to make its workplace riskier. To wit: would not UPS at least double its profits by raising the number of its violations to 372 for 1998? Could not it fairly triple or quadruple its profits by budgeting for and investing penalty amounts of $1.2 million or $1.8 million in fiscal years 1999 and 2000?

By considering my simple proposal, corporations like UPS and others will guarantee that the United States remains a vibrant economic dynamo of a country.

What I need to confess is I didn't sign my name to these ravings, attributing them instead to one "Gary Pike": local firebrand, all-American crank, and, yes, fictional creation. I wrote regularly for the newspaper as Pike—and other characters besides—concealing myself behind various free e-mail accounts. Oh, how many are there? About as many accounts, each constructing and sustaining one separate identity, as months I had spent working there full time. You can always depend on a counterfeiter for a fancy prose style. My spare time I employed in the manufacture of whole companies. They emerged from my head wildly profitable and fully staffed, with ambitious assistants obeying the bidding of sage bosses. If my fictional characters filed tax returns, I probably would have been personally responsible for creating more new jobs in central New York than any non-fictional company.

I littered my fictions with references, allusions, and bastardized quotations from literature, less to show whence I had come than to underline how utterly irrelevant it now all seemed. I quoted Donald Barthelme but made the words pass through the dead lips of Adam Smith. Having just read *Mason & Dixon*, I inserted the opinions of T.R. Pynchon, knowingly citing him as an American historian and author of the monograph *A Most Intoxicating Liquid: A History of Coffee, the Coffee Bean, and Coffee Houses in Pre-Revolutionary America*. In another counterfeit, I drew names of characters from a *New York Review of Books* essay about Vincent van Gogh fakers and the businessmen who knowingly peddled the knockoffs.

As Paul Maliszewski, I continued to report on quarterly figures and tepidly gauge the effects of proposed regulations. My fake characters, however, were free to engage business issues with everything from unhinged speculation to dimwitted appeals to common sense. I granted my characters as many titles ("a consultant for middle-middle and upper-middle managers in the Los Angeles metropolitan area") as tangled points of view and rhetorical tics. I was both pro and con, abstract and specific, rhetorically full of it and full of my fictional selves. In this age of memoir and conspicuous confession, I adopted more than a dozen identities, none of them very truthful but all of them, curiously, found worthy of publication. I was Gary Pike, Samuel Collins, T. Michael Bodine, Carl S. Grimm, Grimm's assistant Simone Fletcher, Noah Warren-Mann, Irving T. Fuller, Daniel Martin, and Pavel R. Liberman, and no one, from the publisher, the editor, and my fellow writers to the advertisers whose ads appeared next to my fictions, ever had a clue.

"In Dow We Trust," *Business Journal of Central New York*, November 10, 1997

To the Editor:

I write this in the wake of the Dow's terrible fall.

Today the Dow fell. Today the Dow fell 550 points. And yet I do not write in sadness, bitterness, anger, or sorrow. Nor do I write to vent my spite or seek my vengeance for that most horrible wrong ever and yet so very routinely brought against the living, the loss of money, spending power, and capital. Rather, I write to pledge my faith to the Dow and to the wisdom of the market for which the Dow stands as a symbolic, statistically real representation. I also write to express anew and loudly even my faith in the Dow as the embodiment of the wealth and economic vigor of this country. Let everyone know: this crash is a test of each of us, investors all. The Dow is merely testing us. To be sure we must respond properly, not with hesitation, indecision, and heartless dalliances with the bond market (woe unto any who dally circumspectly in the bond market!), but with the utmost grace and patience, that rare sort of saintly patience of one who finds real joy in counting money three, four, and five times over again until one is 120 percent positive of the sum total of money in each stack. Today the Dow fell 550 points, and I have only one question: are we or are we not faithful investors? Before you answer, think, for we cannot be merely lukewarm. The Dow will not tolerate lukewarm investors, nor should it.

Of only one thing can we be certain: the Dow has fallen before and it will fall again. I was recently invited by the *Syracuse Post-Standard* to contribute my thoughts for its coverage of the tenth anniversary of Black Monday, another day that tested our collective faith in the market. While the paper chose to run a report from one of the wire services instead of the local story, readers may be interested in my comments, particularly in light of today's small corrective crash.

I remember well October 19, 1987. I recall watching in grim, unabashed terror as the Dow plunged to new lows. So low. I had tried periodically during the day to reach my broker. The phone, I realized epiphanically, perhaps for the first time though I can't be sure, was the instrument by which I can reach the Dow and communicate my instructions to it. But not that afternoon and not that day. I wanted to sell, but couldn't get through, couldn't, in fact, get any answer. I called and called, but the Dow said nothing in return, answering only in silence and the mocking tone of a busy signal. In retrospect, I am glad I did not sell. I am glad I stuck by the market, continued to invest vigorously, and maintained the level of my faith in the Dow.

In wars nobody ever reports the good news. This truth is no less true of the days when financial markets result in ruin for some people. Few reporters reported the small recoveries during the day. Do you know on Black Monday, the Dow climbed between eleven and a little after noon and again after one and once more just before three o'clock? Few do. Why does nobody speak of these recoveries? Surely in today's crash, the same is true. Were you to sit down and plot the Dow's movements over fifteen- to thirty-minute intervals, the story would be more complicated, far richer even than is contained in the word "crash." Remember that in recoveries there is hope, even in small ones. All recoveries, even less-than-one-point upticks, contain signs spoken directly to the faithful and audible to those awake to hear. (Those who can discern while blindfolded a one-dollar bill from a twenty by the sounds they make certainly know of what I speak.)

The year before Black Monday, my wife and I bought my son stocks for his birthday. We selected for the boy's very first investment Microsoft—a small number so as not to spoil him. That year everyone in an investing way was excited about Microsoft, and besides, my son showed an early, heartwarming interest in the workings of computers, particularly the creation of clever, memory-resident, Windows-based applications for those working in home-office business environments. My son, it also must be said, shares with Microsoft CEO Bill Gates a birthday, October 28. Tomorrow, coincidentally enough. (But in this age of the Dow may anything rightly be said to be a coincidence?)

We couldn't just buy the boy stocks for his birthday, however. For how long and loudly would he have howled at that rough, unkind outrage? He's a boy, after all. So my wife and I bought him a basketball to go with the stocks.

The evening of the crash I telephoned my son at school, and I said to him, "Son, the Dow has crashed, son. Your basketball's now worth more than your stock." This was, of course, a bit of an exaggeration on my part, though Microsoft stock did drop 19.25 points to 45.25 by the close of trading that day.

The value of a thing is determined only by a buyer and a seller who find a price which both believe agreeable. The faiths of the buyer and seller support this value. Even after today's crash, the value of all shares on the New York Stock Exchange is more than $8 trillion. It is estimated that $2 trillion of this value was added in the last year during the Dow's meteoric rise to the highest heights it has known. Similarly, the value of the economy may be calculated by the price of the goods and services it produces. This year that value is approximately $7 trillion. Since the economy grew less than 4 percent last year, it may be said that the value of goods and services added in the last year is $280 billion. Only realists and fools dare to suggest that because $280 billion is less than one-seventh of the increase in claims on the stock exchange, the Dow and the market that it embodies are grossly inflated in value. Realists and fools are of no concern to investors, those individuals who move adroitly in the dark, guided by faith, those who sustain the market with their belief in the market. Today the Dow fell 550 points. I write to ask each of you to maintain along with me your faiths in the Dow.

—Gary Pike, Syracuse, New York

On Tuesdays before an issue of the newspaper went to the printer, Norman Poltenson, the publisher of the *Business Journal*, would give me his latest editorial for proofreading and comment. The rest of the paper was usually complete but for a yawning white space reserved for him on page four. His byline and a short note about upcoming personal appearances (such as a minute or so weekly on a local TV news broadcast, at 6:45 A.M.) would already be laid out and, along with the other pages, hanging on either side of a long, narrow hallway for staff inspection. Poltenson's picture, a heavily shaded pencil drawing that I thought of as a distant and very poor cousin of those copper-plate engravings in the *Wall Street Journal*, would look down from the top of the third column, surveying the thirty column inches of nothingness.

Poltenson the man would be upstairs in his office, writing to exact length. He was more familiar with printing than writing and took a kind of pedantic pride in converting the number of unfilled column inches on page four into a frighteningly close approximation of the number of words required, all in his head. Poltenson had come to publish the newspaper not as a writer or an editor but as the inheritor of his family's printing business, which he and his brother decided to sell. Starting the newspaper consumed most of Norman's share of the proceeds; buying a competing newspaper (in order to put it out of business) took care of the rest. By the time I began working at the *Business Journal*, the paper reached about nine thousand readers in sixteen counties across central and upstate New York—business owners mostly, whose names were culled from a Dun & Bradstreet database and who received their subscriptions gratis. It was the ideal journalistic stepping stone to not much of anything. Despite its considerable pretensions, all that it had in common with the *Wall Street Journal* was the word "journal."

When he finished his latest editorial, Poltenson would come looking for me. "Mr. Maliszewski," he would say, "if you would be so kind as to read this over and offer your comments to me with your usual alacrity, I would appreciate it." For the next half hour I would grind my teeth and stomp my feet and pound my desk over howlers like "Any attempt to 'humanize' the corporation should be dismissed as syrupy, corrosive sentiment" and broken-back beauties like "Oh, and if you break out murders from general crime, businesspeople were the perps more than 30 percent of the time." Though I'd point out all the holes in his arguments I had the patience to find, Poltenson only seemed to want a thorough proofreading. He would listen patiently as I expressed my disbelief that, say, mutual funds were society's great equalizer, but then thank me and accept only my stylistic suggestions.

Out of this climate were born Gary Pike and Samuel Collins. Both debuted in the same issue, writing in response to a predictable Poltenson editorial decrying regulations created by OSHA, his *bête noire*. All the covert ideological cargo Poltenson slipped by on a raft of ill-gotten statistics, Pike would hail loudly as righteous and true. Collins wrote only on those occasions when I was so angry I couldn't be bothered to invent a satirical perspective.

As the fake letters became more frequent and windier, the white space available to Poltenson dwindled. Finally, one of Pike's letters managed to kick Poltenson off the page altogether. This was not good. Although I enjoyed seeing the editorial page, always home to dozens of statistical fictions, become a venue for my real fiction, it bothered me that my counterfeits allowed Poltenson to skip out on a column or two. Clearly, I had to change tactics. My characters would need to become full-fledged contributors to the *Business Journal* by developing their own subjects and making forays into expert columns and perhaps even the news section, a kind of promised land for the faker.

As my hackwork piled still higher, I began to think of journalism not as a series of unique assignments or stories, but as a limited number of ideas and conventions, which each story had somehow to affirm. When Poltenson assigned me to write about tort reform legislation proposed by New Yorkers for Tort Reform, a faux-grassroots effort led by major manufacturers, he suggested I interview a few of the reformers, talk to a trial lawyer, and then write it up with the usual on-one-hand-on-the-other-hand equivocation. In the hands of a trained journalist, such back-and-forth disagreements write themselves and can be as long or short as the editorial requirements of the moment. But such a standard telling of the story also includes little or no context or historical perspective, and the reader is left with nothing but a sense of muddled ambivalence. Every story's a toss-up.

But after looking into New Yorkers for Tort Reform, I decided to write about the survey they had commissioned, showing how outrageously worded questions were the basis of the group's results. I had only recently started to work at the paper and had unfortunately not yet mastered the forms. Poltenson slugged the story as "analysis," which seemed to me like an apology or a warning label. Analysis, I gathered, was not one of the traditional forms at the *Business Journal*. As I learned to stop worrying and love the forms, I also came to appreciate their efficiency. No matter how contrary and damning the information I unearthed in interviews and research, a couple of turns of the crank insured that it all came out looking as indistinguishable as the next story—and the next story and the next story.

When I heard about the *New Republic* writer Stephen Glass, I thought I had found a coconspirator. Here, maybe, was someone else who understood the restrictions of journalism and bristled against them. I earnestly wrote him an e-mail care of his last-known fake company. I described my project as a series of necessary counterfeits and expressed the sincere hope that he too had a satirist's motives. At magazines and newspapers, meanwhile, the hand-wringing and soul-searching went into high gear. Presses all along the eastern seaboard turned out one disingenuous apology after another. Forgive us, readers. This won't happen again. Editors came in for light scoldings and smacks across their wrists. Contrite tenders of the journalistic flame suggested that perhaps the young writers should be kept from writing articles with unnamed sources, a signature of the Glassian style. They're not old enough to use the power tools, people implied.

After spending most of a weekend reading the collected works of Stephen Glass, I decided his writing was not so much satiric as sarcastic. Not a single article tweaked readers' expectations or questioned received opinion. He was no faker. He only made the conventionally wise seem that much wiser, and was nothing more than a master of journalism's simple forms, a kind of super-freelancer. Men's magazines, policy magazines—to Glass they were all just magazines. His writing carefully mimicked the style and form of each one, bowing obsequiously to everything its editors valued. The articles hit all the right targets and confirmed all the right stereotypes. Ever think stockbrokers pay too much attention to Alan Greenspan's every utterance? A Glass article confirms what you suspected, inventing an investment company where the traders pray before a photograph of Chairman Al. Stay up late fretting over the vast right-wing conspiracy to get the president? Glass reports on one so literal it should have been called "The Right-Wing Conspiracy."

Glass's articles were, as commentator after commentator

wrote, too good to be true, but that hardly explains why they were published. Editors didn't judge them good articles because they were well written or moving. They ran Glass's writing because it did everything that good writing in the *New Republic* is expected to do. A Glass article told you that what you assumed was, in fact, true—young Republicans are visigothic—and it slyly congratulated you on the intelligence of your suspicions. The combination of colorful tales buttressing cherished assumptions was so potent that everyone who came into contact with his stories desperately wanted them to be true, and so printed them.

The *Business Journal* approached stories with exactly the same logic. News stories, for instance, followed several hardened formulas, each affiliated with a popular fictional genre: the merge and acquisition (best written using the techniques of a romance novel, with the central metaphor of a wedding); the company under investigation (refer to John Grisham's legal thrillers, casting the company as an innocent yet scrappy underdog); the CEO with an unlikely or nontraditional background (fairy tale); the quarterly report disclosing surprisingly strong/weak earnings (vignette, tuned to frequencies of sweetness or sadness, as appropriate); the bankruptcy (tragedy, mournfully rehearsing the age-old verity that a marketing budget is not to be trifled with); the profile of an eccentric (screwball comedy, starring a renegade businessman who walked away from his six-figure salary as a vice president of marketing only to turn to manufacturing decorative mailboxes and—would you believe?—marketing them through mail-order catalogs).

A fictional expert like Carl S. Grimm, who began writing

columns for the *Business Journal* in January 1998, appears like any other dispenser of corporate advice. He follows the rules of the genre. He is casually confident yet serious. He possesses bold, counterintuitive ideas but remains well versed in the deployment of clichés. His background mixes equal parts intrigue and prestige: "A former official with both the State Department and CIA, Grimm frequently speaks at overseas engagements for the U.S. Agency for International Development, Andersen Consulting, the American Federation of Independent Businesses, and Carnival Cruise Lines' Business Traveler Adventure series." He's independent. He's successful. His book, *Living Liquidly: How Being More Like Money Pays Off*, will be published by HarperCollins.

What an amazing life Grimm seemed to lead. To crisscross borders and time zones in solitary pursuit of accumulating the most money possible was certainly close to the unacknowledged dreams of many readers of the *Business Journal*. Were they not regrettably bound to this earth and these flabby bodies, to mortgaged homes and long-term leases on Sevilles, they could surely follow in Grimm's footsteps. Failing that, readers could cozy up to his columns, turning to the warm words of an accomplished expert for the moral instruction and diversion traditionally found in genre fiction.

"Toward a Life of Pure, 100% Liquidity," *Business Journal of Central New York*, July 6, 1998

Carl S. Grimm is a consultant specializing in currency and trade opportunity analysis, foreign risk assessment, industry informational surveys, and market share projection specification programs, a service that applies the strengths of multimedia, computer-aided design in three dimensions, and fully interactive technologies to the challenges of forecasting business and global patterns of change.

I suppose the day was like any other, really. I found myself on the helicopter from LaGuardia to Kennedy, endeavoring to bypass the traffic by flying over the city instead of having to try to have some people fight my way through it. With total lapsed time well shy of ten minutes, the cloudless skies of postcards, and no symptoms of incipient motion sickness, I was, I must admit, making quite an embarrassing success of it. Along for the ride—in addition to the pilot, whose name I forget—was my new friend, whom I'll call "Marvin." Poor "Marvin." As Manhattan, history's best real estate deal, heaved into sight off to our left, I was commiserating with "Marvin," who confided in me how he found himself completely unable to live on $450,000 per year. He had, he claimed, done everything right: was educated at a private prep school in Connecticut where the halls are decorated with portraits of past students who became presidents and the classes are attended by young presidents-to-be; graduated Harvard with honors and Harvard Law at the very top of his class; was offered positions with more Wall Street firms than he had fingers to count; and made partner and then senior partner sooner even than his ambitious life-schedule had stipulated. Yet here he was, he said, flat broke and bumming a ride on my helicopter. Strangely, I knew exactly what he meant.

It was later that same day, as the more memorable pieces of my conversation with "Marvin" bounced and rolled around inside my head like so many shiny coins tossed by well-wishers into a public fountain, that I vowed to achieve a life of pure 100 percent liquidity in order to avoid the fate of "Marvin" and that wretched existence of his. To do so, I had only to make over myself in the image and essential character of money. On my flight to Jakarta, a few people sat haloed by the harsh dome lights, studying *FEER*, the *Far Eastern Economic Review*, and the recently collected reports of the IMF. While most everyone else in first class curled up with the peach-colored pages of the *Financial Times* or rested behind the satin sleep masks provided by the airline, I found sufficient think-time to revise my long-term goals, rearranging and reprioritizing. I added one more: Be as liberated as capital itself.

What is the liquid life?

We all know what we mean when we talk of money or capital as liquid wealth; its properties allow it to be applied anywhere for any purpose by anyone who has it. It was Adam Smith, the economist and proto-warrior for free trade, who so presciently wrote, "The practiced accumulation of capital is the topmost taper on the golden candelabrum of existence." Capital, Smith knew, is easily transferable and more widely accepted than a Visa card. (On a Caribbean cruise I once heard that foreign peoples will treat a U.S. dollar with the awe of an alien landing.) The liquid life has in common with money this freedom of movement. The purely liquid among us are always already willing to move—and move quickly. Liquid-lifers find work instead of allowing work to find them. It's a way of traveling light, acting fast, and staying one step ahead. People of pure liquid move to where it suits them best; they relentlessly seek their level.

Close readers of these pages will no doubt remember my

last letter, which projected handsome, if embarrassing, profits in the welfare management industry, what I called the welfare of welfare. When I wrote that letter five months ago, I was living in Philadelphia. Now I'm in Chicago and in between I've probably lived in three or four more places besides. Perhaps "lived" is not the proper word for what I do, because I stay in hotels, luxury hotels to be sure, the sort of places where the televisions are not chained to the floor, places at which my arrival is eagerly anticipated, my needs met and micromanaged by people employed by people managed by other people who acquired hotel/restaurant degrees, and my departure widely mourned. But since I'm never anywhere for very long, perhaps even "stay" implies too great a sense of permanence. Really, I light from assignment to assignment, providing billable advice as I go. I move from hotel to hotel, from Hilton to Holiday Dome to Radisson to Adam's Mark to Hilton again. I hardly disturb anything but the air around me, I displace so very little volume. I am like the white aphid on the bottom of the red rose petal.

The liquid life is a state of mind, really. Sure there are modest costs, e.g., take the wife, who didn't feel she wanted to accompany me on my quest to obtain the liquid life, though she did try it for a while (one month, not to her liking). She feared super liquidity is what it is. And then one of my daughters left home to become a model and now she's just outside of Milan, working, where some magazine or other wrote her up as the Ivanka Trump of the spring season. Her roommate has been called the Ivanka Trump of her generation. The other daughter, younger and sweet, is in a special school in Switzerland.

An example should bring the liquid state of mind into

sharper focus. Follow the money in this quote from the *Financial Times*: "The return of the capital that fled after Beijing's missile tests in the Taiwan Straits in March last year, a relatively accommodating liquidity policy by the central bank and active buying by government-controlled funds have brought doubled share values in little more than a year." First of all, congratulations are in order—way to go, Taiwan. But let's follow the money, shall we? The money was afraid of political fallout from Chinese missile tests. Fair enough, money fled. Money went elsewhere. Money canceled lucrative, but tentative, deals, turned tail, and just plain left. Money hopped jets with departing businesspeople or rode electronic wires and flew, flew away, trailing more zeroes than you or maybe I can imagine through the money-sphere. But then you can see what happened next. There's a happy ending here. Money returned. Money marched back into Taiwan like conquering soldiers. Money came home to Mom.

So what's this all mean? you ask. When I speak of the liquid life, I speak of a life that abides by the rules of money. If you can do better, be better, and achieve more elsewhere, why then, by gosh, *be* there, *go* there, *now*. Karl Marx had it only partially right. Labor and capital *do* obey two unique sets of rules. But Marx could not have foreseen the likes of me and the few people like me. He could not have imagined the way we make airports our living rooms, and their long, glassed-in concourses our entryways. That's us on the phone, conducting business on our laps. That's us playing solitaire, always solitaire, on color laptop computers, or taking a chance on the video poker machines that lean down over bars like forlorn women waiting for companions. We go where the money goes, to the new lands of opportunity and investment, looking for financial milk and honey. Here again is Smith, north star to any thinking economist: "Opportunity is the hearty, weathered sailor on the tumultuous seas of loss and gain." We liquid types go how money goes, by air, at cruising altitudes of 12,000 feet or more, and in first class, baby. Be fearless, be quick, be liquid. Who are we? We are the willfully and meaningfully and lucratively transient, living by silence, exile, cunning—and so on. We always shop duty-free.

What's the opposite of the liquid life?

Four words: routine, attachment, sedentary, and homebody, or R.A.S.H. The opposite of the liquid life is a solid one, and solidity is produced by the above four behaviors. Worst of all, solidity causes a rash. A real specter is haunting America at the end of the millennium—the specter of solidity. Remember: solidity is the nightmare from which we are trying to awake. But what happened to "Marvin"? you ask. "Marvin" did not live the right life. Poor "Marvin." He was too heavy and entirely too solid. Regrettably, his occupation, the law, drew him back to earth. The law is fundamentally concerned with representing the legal considerations of bodies, people or corporations. The law is by definition a material pursuit, uses material means to achieve material remedies. Far better to be like money, I say, and trade in information.

Poor "Marvin," he couldn't move like money moves. He didn't even seem to recognize himself in my description of the law. When last I saw him, in Kennedy, he merely looked fed up and annoyed, no doubt angry with himself. Clearly, he appreciated the wisdom in everything I had so unselfishly shared with him about the liquid life, while both on the helicopter and the ground, during the hour or so after that I walked around after him wherever he went. "Marvin" was not and would never be liquid, but he at least was aware of the liquid life. He said to me, "Carl S. Grimm, I wish I never asked you for a ride." I had dealt him a rude epiphany and naturally he felt he'd have been better off not knowing. He knew he was unable to follow me into 100 percent liquidity. He could never be me, and so when I ducked into the men's room to avail myself of the soft soap and hand towels, he saw his opportunity and he ran. Upon exiting, I spied only his flapping coattails more than five gates away. What did I do? you ask. I gave chase. Could he not even face me? Winded, I stopped and yelled out his real name. I needed to assure him his failure was not a problem. To this day I can still see how he turned, shook his head in despair and, waving to me feebly, took off again. With awareness comes much sadness.

I've often wondered what it would be like to encounter *Gulliver's Travels* without having any prior knowledge about the book or its author. What if it could be published as a guidebook and shelved in the travel section among all the Fodor's guides and Lonely Planets? Tear off the prefaces by the editors, take away the inevitable essay by Allan Bloom, peel back the thin slices of footnotes, and you'd be left with a book that not only fits the form of the travel guide, but that fiendishly parodies it as well. The book's first two editions tellingly carried Gulliver as its author. Swift was absent from the title page.

Believing that satire requires a certain amount of intentional mislabeling, I set out to translate the text of a torture manual used at the School of the Americas into the language and rhetoric of a manager's how-to. With very few changes—substituting "employee" for "subject," for instance—the piece began to look more and more like an advice column. Now published and with nothing whatsoever to announce it as satire, it lies in wait, looking and reading like just another article. In the *Business Journal* it is oddly at home.

"Don't Get Caught Being a Weak Manager," *Business Journal of Central New York*, November 10, 1997

T. Michael Bodine is a partner, senior business-to-business consultant and vice president of marketing, West Coast Operations with Universal Business Consultants (UBC), a full-service instructional and consultative "academy" for business owners and managers. UBC offers nine levels of advanced intensive coursework and customized, on-site workshops, publishes the Universal Business Consultants Newsletter (UBCN) for subscribing alumni, and currently has offices in Los Angeles, London, Honolulu, and Hong Kong.

As a long-time consultant and instructor of middle-middle and upper-middle-managers in the Los Angeles metropolitan area, I've seen my fair share of problems. But no manager is ever beyond help. As I gaze back on my years, the number one problem that sticks out in my mind about my business is weak managers. If "weak manager" appeared in Webster's Dictionary (the fact is that it doesn't, *yet*), I have a feeling it would be defined as "one who rarely or only inconsistently applies adequate force behind his managerial hand." In my advanced courses as well as in my publications I emphasize a set of lessons that are easy to learn and even easier to apply.

First of all, the manager must learn to use coercion effectively. Coercion might sound like a dirty word, but I request your patience in considering its usefulness to managers the world over. The fundamental rule of coercion is that its purpose is to induce psychological regression in an employee by bringing a superior force from outside to bear on his will to resist, resulting in a more effective managerial style. Regression of this sort is basically a controlled loss of autonomy and is marked by the return to an earlier behavioral level. As an employee regresses, his learned personality traits have been described as falling away in reverse chronological order. Destructive capacities such as ironic detachment or a regard for one's self are lost. With practice, an employee + coercion will = a worker.

Always remember that an employee's sense of identity depends on a continuity in his surroundings, habits, appearance, relations with others, etc. Always remember too what I call the 4 C's of good managing: Careful Coercion Corrodes Continuity. An example: an employee's desk is an extension of his body, and the manager should look closely at the artifacts of the desk for hints at the weakest part of that body. Pictures of children and loved ones might point to the family. Postcards from last summer's vacation point to the importance of leisure. Stuffed animals surely signify a need to be hugged, even loved. Managers, make careful note of these observations.

Now disrupting an employee's continuity can always be a productive method of applying managerial pressure. Detention and a deprivation of sensory stimuli are two methods which on the surface sound draconian, but which can, on second look, be easily adapted for the workplace. Allow me to illustrate. Detention can mean arriving early and staying late.

Contrive ways to keep an employee by your side all day, perhaps by making appointments with the target employee early in the morning and around 4 P.M., when "quitting time-itis" has been known to set in among some. Depriving sensory stimuli can be accomplished with embarrassing ease: take away an employee's radio.

I have been suggesting some possible actions for the weak manager. In some cases actions are best, but in other cases perhaps only the threat of action is enough. I always impress on the managers in my courses that they internalize the difference between threats suggested and threats enacted. Remember a rule I call "Follow through is up to you." Bear in mind that the threat of coercion usually weakens or destroys resistance more effectively than coercion itself. Just as an example, one having nothing to do with actual workplace conduct, the threat to inflict pain can trigger fears far more damaging than the immediate sensation of pain. And anyway, sometimes pain causes a sense of hopelessness, nihilism, and despair that is too bleak even to be useful to managers who are experts in these techniques. A reminder: this example has nothing to do with actual conduct in the workplace.

While on the subject of coercion, I would be remiss if I didn't mention my experience with hypnosis. I have had some indescribable personal success with the hypnotic arts. Allow me to describe. Though it's true that answers obtained from an employee under the influence of hypnotism are highly suspect, as they are often based upon the suggestions of the manager and are distorted or fabricated, hypnosis does have its clear benefits and I remain one of its vocal champions. An employee's strong desire to escape the stress of the situation can create a state of mind called "heightened suggestibility." The manager can then take advantage of this state of mind by creating a situation in which an employee will cooperate because he believes he has been hypnotized. This hypnotic situation can be created using a "magic room" technique.

For example, imagine that an employee is given a hypnotic suggestion that his hand is growing warm. This being the "magic room," his hand actually does become warm, with the aid of a bi-level, rheostat-controlled diathermy machine previously concealed in the arm of the special office chair. Further, an employee may be given a suggestion that a cigarette will taste bitter and then be given a cigarette prepared to have a slight but noticeably bitter taste.

In view of the litigious nature of U.S. society today, being a business owner and an employer of people has never been more difficult. The bad news is it probably won't get easier any time soon. The good news is that there are things you can do, as a manager or business owner, that you probably haven't tried yet. Bear this in mind.

While there is no drug that can force every employee to divulge all the information he has, in a state of heightened suggestibility and in a duly-outfitted "magic room," a placebo such as a harmless sugar pill can have extravagant effects. The manager can tell an employee (already in the right frame of mind, of course) that the placebo was a truth serum that will make him want to talk and prevent all his lying. Things grow complicated here and can fast become overheated, psychologically speaking, but the end result is that the employee will indeed talk, as it's clearly his only avenue of escape from a depressing situation. He will want to believe that he has been drugged because then nobody can blame him for telling his entire story. A mere sugar pill provides him with the rationalization he needs to cooperate. The manager will keep a number of these sugar pills handy.

I have mentioned some of the more powerful techniques used to create a useful state of regression. Sometimes, however, the manager should consider more subtle means, such as:

Manipulation of time
Retarding and advancing clocks
Offering free meals at odd times
Disrupting sleep schedules with either early morning or
    late night "emergency" calls
Unpatterned and aimless questioning sessions
Vigorous nonsensical questioning
Ignoring halfhearted attempts to cooperate
Rewarding non-cooperation
Arbitrary body language

Surely I have suggested that there remains a wide and plentiful universe of options available to the manager who possesses an open mind.

One cubicle away, my managing editor was on the telephone trying to reach a prospective freelance writer who had materialized out of the vast wasteland of New York's north country. "I need a number for Noah Warren-Mann," he told an operator. A query letter had arrived from Noah recently, bearing story ideas aplenty, and my managing editor was apparently eager to speak with the man whose e-mail messages, rich in parentheticals and exclamation points, conveyed a passion for business and an aspiration to join the team. ("That's Warren *hyphen* Mann.") I knew a bit about Noah. ("Could you look under 'Mann' too?") I knew he had no phone, for instance, and that every wildcard search would come up empty. ("You checked Felt Mills *and* Watertown?") I knew this because Noah Warren-Mann was I.

Born and bred in humble Watertown, New York, Noah was an up-and-coming young businessman who dreamed of the high-tech, gadget-galore life he had read about in *Wired* and *Fast Company* and was committed to achieving it in his home-town: a city known, if at all, as the origin of the ubiquitous pine tree–shaped air freshener. While Noah had what high school guidance counselors charitably call "potential" and "enthusi-asm," his best efforts produced MicroVisions, a one-man com-puter maintenance company that still fit comfortably in the trunk of a small car. True, Watertown barely sustained Noah's most micro of visions and, true, he didn't have a telephone, but the newspaper held him in high regard anyway and published his first article, "Upstate Businesses Recover Slowly from Wicked Ice Storm." Only the ice storm was real.

After paying his dues with such mundane reporting, the stage was set for Noah's star turn. He would profile Telopera-tors Rex, Inc., a homegrown company with the revolutionary idea of using people to answer telephones. After a number of editorial delays, having nothing to do with the story's utter lack of veracity, "TRI Brings On-Call Phone Personnel to the North Country" ran in the June 8, 1998 issue of the *Business Journal*. The headline stretched across the top of two inside pages.

The published article delivered exciting glimpses of the habits and musings of TRI's principal, one Irving T. Fuller. In tones of breathless awe, Noah described the owner's lifelong but utterly irrelevant fascination with dinosaurs and, like any good profiler, used detail to offer Tinkertoy psychological insights into his entrepreneurial epiphany (a young Irv standing before a *T. rex*) and resulting character:

> Today, there are large framed prints of a triceratops, an archaeopteryx, and a deltadromeus on the walls of Fuller's office in Watertown, along with movie posters from *Jurassic Park* and *The Lost World*. On an antique mahogany credenza behind him, pictures of his wife and three children share space with a close-up photo of a stegosaurus skull and an artist's rendering of a brachiosaurus—a slow, gentle-seeming herbivore—in muted pastel tones. A cleverly painted plaster cast of a thigh-bone sits propped up against the back wall of his office, flanking a large picture window on one side, with the U.S. flag on the other. The bone easily stands floor to ceiling, with one panel of the acoustic drop ceiling moved aside so that it continues on up into the wiring and the dark. The replica, he says, was cast in a limited edition from the *Rex* held by the Museum of Natural History, the very skeleton that long ago fired Fuller's imagination.

Naturally, Noah was as eager to explain Fuller's "Darwinian" philosophy of management as he was to tell us about his phone-answering system: "A recent memo to inspire the marketing staff began, 'First, let's cogitate like the advanced primates we supposedly are. Personally, I gave up thinking like a lizard, and you should, too.' " We counted ourselves lucky to sit at the feet of this impressive thinker and merely collect his pearls:

> Evolution is not, as some people believe, about the changes oc-
> curring in organisms due to adaptation, natural selection, and
> other forces that are so minute and gradual as to be not directly
> observable given their long-term nature. It's really about not
> missing the next big thing. It's about adapting yourself and
> modeling yourself and rigorously remaking yourself quickly
> enough in order to embody the next big thing before it's even
> big. Evolution is about electing to survive.

"Fuller" was so pleased with Noah's bouquet that he decided to excerpt it on the company's Web site. He also created a media kit around the glowing profile and, in the hope of reaching a broader audience, sent it to journalists at local television stations and daily newspapers.

Web sites, as we all know, are crucial to reaching that anonymous, broader audience. TRI's site (which a later news article described as "very professional") was in fact designed and placed online in a single night by my brother. We spent no money and settled on a simple aesthetic: appropriate and cobble together the gaudy dreck of non-fictional corporate Web pages. Like medieval alchemists, we sought to transmute their crap into TRI's gold plating. A pseudo-Celtic symbol, chosen more for its size than any particular meaning, became the perfect corporate logo for a company declaring itself "Your choice for the new millennium." AT&T's and MCI's Web sites coughed up all manner of generic images of telephones and operators. Stock photographs used to fancy up especially thin year-end reports did wonders for TRI's image. An animated Hewlett-Packard banner ad, after a little doctoring, crowed about TRI's Vetracom 2000: "Simply . . . let us answer your telephone." The Web site showcased non-news (Look, new Web site!) and the trophies of a year's invented successes (opportunities in Europe and an economic development grant courtesy of Governor Pataki). All very professional, indeed.

I didn't really expect local journalists, once they received the media kit, which included Noah's profile and a sheaf of press releases, to perpetuate the TRI hoax. I figured its days were numbered. Readers in Watertown had, after all, informed the *Business Journal* just days after Noah's article ran that there was no Fuller, no TRI, no Noah, anywhere. What I did expect was that people would look at the Web site, the stack of fake press releases, the profile, and realize, without my prompting, that TRI—which clearly doesn't exist—was a lot like other, real businesses, with their own very professional Web sites, press releases, and hagiographic profiles. That this, to put it simply, was a satire.

And, indeed, the reporters who contacted TRI by e-mail were definitely wandering in the country of humor. "Congratulations," a reporter in Syracuse wrote. "It was a fun read." Another, based in Albany, enthused: "Your George E. Pataki press release was dead-on. Most of it reads exactly the same way the stuff from the gov's office does. . . . Also, I must tell you, the governor's chief press spokesman is not amused."

Within three days of being mailed, the media kits generated articles in the *Syracuse Post-Standard* and the *Watertown Daily Times*, and WSTM-TV3 ran a story about TRI during both of its evening newscasts. Contrary to the headlines and reporting in the Watertown and Syracuse newspapers ("Faux Fax Creates Scramble, Query" and "Fax Too Good to Be True," respectively), I sent no fax. Someone, perhaps at a state agency, perhaps an editor or reporter, took distribution into his own hands. Both newspapers then were reporting on the effects of the media's own subsequent, wider circulation of my humble media kit. But instead of the engaging discussion of satire I'd prepared for, the reporters focused on TRI as a byzantine flim-flam. Setting the tone of the coverage, each article quoted the governor's press secretary, who said, "This falls into the realm of the bizarre," adding, in one account, "It's clearly inappropriate." Eager to lend seriousness to the story, both articles also raised the specter of a government investigation, with the Watertown newspaper suggesting that TRI's media kit had provoked widespread panic: "The counterfeit press release had gubernatorial and legislative press aides scrambling to figure out what was going on, and Attorney General Dennis C. Vacco's office is now investigating." State officials did not speculate about TRI's motives, but the *Business Journal*'s managing editor plied local reporters with suggestions of "some kind of elaborate business scam at the heart" of the hoax.

The real scam was the way reporters spun the press releases into news. I was pleased to note how the reporters lifted my own strategic phrasings. The Syracuse story—about 40 percent of which was taken word for word from the media kit—concluded with three lengthy quotations from my fake press releases, my Governor Pataki, and my state senator.

After a few days, a few articles, and a bewildered editorial warning against "the potential for electronic scams," the story of TRI expired, the failed yet perplexing swindle of a north country confidence man to the end. Meanwhile, a new misunderstanding was taking shape. It turned out I *was* being investigated. On September 23, 1998, two agents from the state attorney general's office visited me at work (I'd left the *Business Journal* for another job in February) and questioned me for the better part of two hours about TRI and a press release bearing an uncanny resemblance to those issued by Governor Pataki. "Can I call you Paul, or should I call you Noah?" asked the senior member of the duo. My impression was that he had thought of this line at least twenty-four hours earlier.

The investigators were very serious men. They informed me I was looking at possible charges on multiple counts of criminal forgery and some vaguely defined "computer crimes." They gestured ominously and with some pride to two stuffed accordion folders labeled "Press Release." My satire, just more than a page, had blossomed to fill them. It looked like the consequence of being misunderstood was being arrested. My confidence in using irony to communicate was fleeting. If I really had awakened in the land of the literal-minded, then I wanted to be perfectly clear.

So I explained my project as a satire, much as I have here. The officers didn't exactly warm to my apologia. The junior investigator was particularly skeptical, repeatedly scolding me as being morally deficient. He called my project "selfish," the cause of a costly government investigation, and said that what I'd done was like "the guy who sees a weakness in the security of the bank and so robs the bank to prove it can be done instead of using your gifts and intelligence to fix the problem in a straightforward manner." But I persisted. To their insinuations that I was a forger and even insane, I talked about satire and the use of literary pseudonyms. At last, the skeptic asked, "But doesn't satire require that people recognize it as satire?" I took it less as a follow-up question than a signal that, finally, I was being understood.

Then the investigators asked me to commit myself—on paper. I was to provide a statement about my project—no cleverness, no indirection this time. I told them I'd think about what I wanted to say and type something up. I wondered when they needed it by and how many words they wanted. "Look, we're not asking you to go off and make some kind of literary creation," the skeptic shot back. "We want you to sit here and write, by hand, what you did and why." And so I explained it all again, filling several pages with short, unmodified declarative sentences. I larded the statement so heavily with keywords such as "literary," "satire," and "artistic project" that even a summer associate could see that underneath their charges of forgery broiled a First Amendment case, with all the usual media scrutiny and bad publicity.

While I wrote, the officers got down to business with their cell phones. One of them received a call for his partner. Their phones were identical; it seemed they'd accidentally been switched. When I finished writing, the senior officer notarized, signed, and initialed the sheets and had his partner fax them to an attorney. We waited awhile. Then we left my office and went to theirs and waited some more. The attorney, I learned, was to evaluate my written statement, consider the relevant legal statutes, and decide what crimes to have me arrested for. I would be arrested that day, the skeptic assured me. The only question was on what charges.

I found it difficult to eat my lunch. I couldn't imagine keeping my sandwich down. I bit at an apple and polished off my water. We waited some more. Finally, word came back that the attorney did not wish to press charges or make an arrest at this time. At what time would the attorney wish to press charges? I asked. The officers couldn't say. They were going to continue their investigation, they said. Unsure of what exactly there remained to uncover, I asked when they planned on winding this up. Again, they couldn't say for sure. The senior investigator said, "It may be two weeks or it may be two months. The longer it is, the better off you are."

Before saying good-bye, the skeptic had some final advice for me, which I dutifully pass along to any aspiring Swifts: "If you want to be a satirist, get a pen and a pad of paper, write something, and then publish it conventionally. If I open the paper one day and see you're on the *New York Times* bestseller list, then I'll know you're a real satirist."

Despairing of ever living up to the officer's standards and becoming a real writer, I hastily looked to tie up loose narrative threads and conclude my fakes project.

In mid-August the *Business Journal* apologized for the publication of Noah's TRI article, printing "We Apologize," an unsigned notice that was a study in complex obfuscation:

> For twelve years, the *Business Journal* has prided itself on providing the Central New York business community with accurate and useful information, information that our readers rely on to keep them informed about businesses and issues in our region.
>
> On June 8, we fell victim to what now appears to be a hoax, in publishing a freelancer's profile of a relatively young company in the Watertown area.

The apology mentioned only a single fake article and not by name—or should I say, *what now appears to be* a fake article.

Besides publishing sixteen fake letters to the editor and business columns, the paper (read: victim) also knew Noah's other
article was a fake:

> A subsequent phone call from a well-informed reader in Wa-
> tertown sparked our initial suspicions about the story, so we
> immediately began investigating to determine whether the
> story was truth or fiction. Despite repeated attempts, we have
> been unable to make contact with the principals in the firm.

One would, the apology suggested, have to be a well-informed
reader in Watertown to spot the fakery, as if advanced knowledge was necessary, including, perhaps, a proficiency with foreign languages and the ability to converse with natives.

> We were continuing our efforts to resolve our questions about
> the article when we received a mailing from the supposed com-
> pany on August 3. The mailing included a news release that
> appeared to be from Governor George Pataki's office and an-
> nounced that the company had received more than $1 million
> in state economic development grants. We immediately con-
> tacted the state's economic-development arm, Empire State
> Development Corp., to inform officials about the release. In
> fact, it was the *Business Journal*'s call that alerted state officials
> to the apparent escalation of the hoax.

First the victim of a hoax, then the hero of the day? Apparently
this was an apology with a happy ending.

> We regret that we originally published an article that appears
> to be a fabrication. The *Business Journal* prizes its reputation
> for credibility with our readers and strives always to meet or ex-
> ceed their expectations.

What appears to be the *Business Journal*'s apology was not the last word on the fakes. Later I saw the newspaper's editorial/opinion page step boldly into the breach, weighing in several times on the "issue" of fakery and journalism scandals, though always neglecting to mention the paper's close acquaintance with both. In one call to arms, publisher Norman Poltenson blamed journalism scandals on a loose industry not subject to press scrutiny, overrun with people of "a decidedly left-wing slant" and reporters who are "crusaders, out to change society." Three months later the paper's ersatz media critic could only offer thin, homiletic gruel such as "Don't believe anything you hear and only half of what you see"—sternly concluding, "Let the viewer beware!"

But these implicit responses to the apology were preceded by another. Gary Pike, a man of strong opinions and a conservative's conservative, who had last written in with a bit of impressionistic babbitry about the future of shopping malls, was first to accept the paper's apology:

"Apology Accepted," *Business Journal of Central New York*, September 28, 1998

To the Editor:

I write to congratulate the *Business Journal* for having the editorial guts and wherewithal to stand up and apologize to its readers ("We Apologize," August 17, 1998, p. 3). The fact that you are a) able and b) willing to apologize in a straightforward and honest manner, admitting that "what now appears to be a hoax" was published in the newspaper, speaks volumes for you and the kind of work you do. I have no idea to what article you refer, but I nevertheless applaud you for having the integrity to tell us the complete story—you were a victim of another's deceit—and come clean about your minor mistake.

In a year in which many mistakes were made in the name of journalism, from Stephen Glass at the *New Republic* to the African American poet/columnist Patricia Smith and the great Mike Barnicle at the *Boston Globe* to the unnecessary investigation of the corporate practices of the Chiquita Banana Company by a muckraking troublemaker at the *Cincinnati Inquirer*, your incident stands out as being minor and your apology magnanimous. I cannot, of course, speak for all your readers, but, as for this reader, apology accepted. I have been a reader of your newspaper for many years and look forward to many more years of great journalism about this region's business world.

On the same day I read your apology, I later heard President Clinton attempt to apologize to the American people. The two apologies sat down side by side in my mind for the next few days—yours an example of how to do it right and the other a textbook example of extreme disingenuousness and dubious logic. Anyone who tuned in and saw *The Bill Clinton Show* on TV will agree that copping to "a relationship that was inappropriate; in fact, it was wrong" is a far cry from what you say in fewer words and with no misdirection whatsoever. If only our nation's commander-in-chief could have taken a hint from your pages and spoken with one-half the percentage of clarity that permeates through your sentences, as in the following: "We regret that we originally published an article that appears to be a fabrication."

In conclusion, what most cheers me is learning that you investigate yourselves. This reader's mind is put at ease knowing that you investigated the article after publishing it and maintained your efforts even as the principals in the firm apparently aimed to foist their apparent deception on unsuspecting victims. Let it escape nobody's attention, therefore, that it was only because of this newspaper's being literally on the ball that state officials were alerted to the hoax's "apparent escalation." I, for one, can rest easily knowing that you are watching the news and watching yourselves watch the news, acting as both guardian of journalism's lighted torch of truth and the watchdog guarding against journalism's occasional mistakes. Once more, my hat is off to you, my head bowed, and pate exposed.

—Gary Pike, Syracuse, New York

Try as I might, I have not yet managed to write that bestselling work of satire. In the years since, however, several more writers have published fiction as fact. In the pages of the *New Yorker*, Rodney Rothman wrote about walking into a dot-com company and pretending, for seventeen days, that he had a job as a junior project manager. Jay Forman, in *Slate*, told tall tales about fishing for monkeys with fruit as bait. Michael Finkel reported for the *New York Times Magazine* on Youssouf Malé, a young boy forced into a slave's life in Mali and, as it turned out, a composite character created from Finkel's notes and imagination.

All these writers' missteps were as various as their subjects. Rothman neglected to mention that his mother worked briefly at the company where he sat and did nothing. Forman could not, when asked, substantiate that anyone has ever actually gone monkey-fishing, ever. Finkel created a protagonist so that he could render a complex story into one about just a single boy, with one seamless narrative and a nice arc: a clear beginning, middle, and end.

In 2007, the *New Republic* raised questions about the truthfulness of David Sedaris's personal essays. The writer, Alex Heard, argued that Sedaris went "beyond the boundaries of comic exaggeration." Absurd descriptions were one thing, but Sedaris had, as Heard uncovered, embellished his stories. In some cases, he invented anecdotes whole. Commenting on the article for his blog, Daniel Radosh said he was reminded of Rothman's case and thought his misdeeds were no worse than Sedaris's. In many ways, in fact, they were identical. The only difference was that Sedaris, who still writes for the *New Yorker*, was famous, a best-selling author, and Rothman had been a first-time contributor. Rothman wrote Radosh, saying, "When I write nonfiction humor now I try to keep the taking of liberties to a minimum, and I'm as forthcoming as possible about the liberties I do take. I do still occasionally take them." Rothman suggested that humorous nonfiction, like nonfiction storytelling, is a genre that imitates "the way we tell each other good stories orally." When listening to a friend's story or reading a writer's piece of humorous nonfiction, Rothman said, we permit some fudging and forgive some liberties. The real challenge, he added, was in distinguishing between nonfiction storytelling and journalism, where tougher standards must apply. Wrote Rothman:

> In the wake of various mini and major scandals, people understandably push for a firm distinction between them. That

seems like a good idea to me. But my feeling is no matter where you draw the line or how bold the line is, a grey area will always emerge around it. As long as readers want the best, tastiest stories, as they have for a long time, the temptation to elevate story above all other concerns will be too great for the grey area to go away.

For all the differences between these writers—Rothman, Forman, Finkel, and Sedaris—and for all the varieties and degrees of their faking, they make clear that journalism and memoir are games played with a small number of unforgiving forms, that the forms don't always accommodate true stories, that writers sometimes feel urged to fudge, to make the stories fit, and that editors sometimes collude in the process, wittingly or not.

Take Jayson Blair. Blair collected datelines far and wide as a reporter for the *New York Times* while actually staying at home, where, in the comfort of his apartment, he conjured up piquant details to add spice and local color to his articles. Assigned to write about the family of U.S. Army Private Jessica Lynch as they waited to hear word of her rescue, recovery, and return home, Blair imagined a quaint family homestead in rural West Virginia with a porch "overlooking the tobacco fields and cattle pastures," a vista he was so enamored with that he mentioned it twice in the same article. In Blair's world, Lynch's mother, "her eyes red and watery," had "dreamed that her daughter ran away from her unit before the attack to help some Iraqi child." Lynch's father meanwhile spoke, Blair wrote, "about the satellite television service that brought CNN and other cable news networks into his home, his family's long history of military service, and the poor condition of the local economy." Later, the *Times*, attempting to right the many dozens of wrongs in Blair's reporting, discovered no view of fields and pastures, Lynch's mother never had any such dream, and her family doesn't boast a history of military service. Blair wrote five articles about the Lynch family without ever setting foot in West Virginia, and what's more, no member of the family even remembered speaking to him on the phone. Lynch's sister Brandi later told a reporter, "We were joking about the tobacco fields and the cattle." When asked why no one complained about the errors, she said, "We just figured it was going to be a one-time thing."

Unfortunately Blair's embellishments and inventions were only one of many injustices done to the Jessica Lynch story. The Pentagon found in it the makings of a modern myth, an optimistic fable to tell at just the moment when U.S. forces faced unexpected resistance, the path to Baghdad proving more difficult and dangerous than anticipated. The news media, for their part, were more than happy to oblige with heated retellings of the hero's tale. On April 3, 2003, Lynch made the front page of the *Washington Post*. The headline read, "She Was Fighting to the Death," quoting an unnamed official, who added in the article, "She did not want to be taken alive." In official statements, the Pentagon offered dry reports and bland remarks, but behind the scenes and when speaking not-for-attribution, officials elaborated feverishly on the growing body of myth. Lynch, they said, "fought fiercely," emptying her machine gun and killing several Iraqis. She was stabbed and shot multiple times before being captured. Two weeks later, Michael Getler, the *Post*'s ombudsman, sounded a cautionary note about the newspaper's coverage, saying a "more qualified approach" might have been appropriate given "the thin sourcing used," but Getler's article was buried in the second section. Two months later, the *Post* published a more sober account, one less likely to be optioned for an action movie. Lynch was, it turned out, not stabbed or shot. She sustained her injuries when the vehicle she was riding in collided with a jackknifed U.S. truck. In a subsequent ambush, "Lynch tried to fire her weapon, but it jammed." Reflecting on the tale as originally told, the *Post* reporters wrote:

> It became the story of the war, boosting morale at home and among the troops. It was irresistible and cinematic, the maintenance clerk turned woman-warrior from the hollows of West Virginia who just wouldn't quit. Hollywood promised to make a movie and the media, too, were hungry for heroes.

Lynch got her say, finally, when she testified on April 24, 2007, before a House committee holding a hearing about the government's use of misleading information during the wars in Iraq and Afghanistan. "The story of the little girl Rambo from the hills of West Virginia who went down fighting," as Lynch described the oft-told version she heard and read, "was not true." Lynch instead told a third story, unalloyed and plainspoken, which featured logistical nightmares and mechanical failures—not the stuff from which myths are made. Lynch, driving a five-ton water buffalo truck, was part of a hundred-mile-long convoy heading to Baghdad to support the marines already there. But the sand was thick, and her vehicle sank. Lighter, faster vehicles in the convoy pressed on, speeding ahead, but Lynch's truck broke down. She caught a ride with her roommate and they, along with the other slower-moving vehicles in the convoy, continued into al-Nasiriyah. "The vehicle I was riding in was hit by a rocket-propelled grenade and slammed into the back of another truck in our unit," Lynch told the committee. She suffered a six-inch gash to her head and sustained grave injuries to her back and limbs, including a crushed foot and a shattered leg. She received some care at an Iraqi hospital, but it was far from state of the art. Doctors, for example, replaced her femur with a metal rod, made in the 1940s, that was too long. Nurses tried once, without success, to return Lynch to U.S. troops. Later, doctors in Germany found during a physical examination that Lynch had been sexually assaulted. Her injuries, and the pain, are still with her today. "The truth of war is not always easy," Lynch said. "The truth is always more heroic than the hype."

After Blair came one James Frey, who souped up his life and published that edgier, more dangerous version of himself as a memoir, *A Million Little Pieces*, which became a bestseller and a selection in Oprah Winfrey's book club before the book was revealed, by the Smoking Gun, to be a clever mix of muddled memories, bravado, and outright hokum. Stranger yet is the example of JT LeRoy. LeRoy was, we were told, a young writer born in West Virginia of little means and great tragedy. He was saved from a hardscrabble life of homelessness and male prostitution, rose above his abusive circumstances, and achieved cult fame: a hipster Horatio Alger.

Born, it was said, in 1980, JT LeRoy began publishing at the tender age of sixteen. His words, prized for their authenticity and searing honesty, found champions in Michael Chabon,

Winona Ryder, and Bono. Dave Eggers, who contributed an introduction to *Harold's End*, a novella by LeRoy published in 2005, explained that his work is "read and loved, rabidly, by thousands of young and very sensitive people who believe that JT speaks for them." Eggers predicted, "JT Leroy's first two books, *Sarah* and *The Heart Is Deceitful Above All Things*, will prove to be among the most influential American books of the last ten years." Later that year, an investigative exposé in *New York* magazine revealed that LeRoy's books—all of his writing, really—were in fact an act of literary ventriloquism by Laura Albert, a forty-year-old woman from Brooklyn who, notably, had never been to West Virginia and who invented LeRoy, in all his misery, using him as a pseudonym and an attention-getting persona. The books have, if anything, proven to be more infamous than influential.

Before Albert was unmasked, she managed to fool readers and editors and journalists and reviewers alike. One such editor was Marc Smirnoff, who published an article by LeRoy about Loretta Lynn in the *Oxford American*'s 2005 Music Issue. LeRoy's appeal, to Smirnoff and others, relied on equal parts pity for his tough life and desire for his hipster cool. "He was a lyricist for a nasty-sounding San Francisco band called Thistle," Smirnoff writes in "Anatomy of a Hoaxing," his searching apologia and attempt to understand the LeRoy phenomenon and his own complicity in it. "Everything about the twenty-five-year-old hipster sounded very, very cool." LeRoy's writing, Smirnoff said, "bustled with an irresistible exuberance." He adds, "Also, the can't-turn-away-from-the-car-wreck minutiae of LeRoy's life with his stripper mother were bound to rouse the sedentary."

Albert invited many people to attend and view that car

wreck, and few, it seems, passed on the opportunity. In his hey-day, LeRoy was profiled in the Style pages of the *New York Times*, contributed a travel article about Disneyland Paris to the newspaper, guest-edited Da Capo's *Best Music Writing* collection, and saw his work anthologized in *The Best American Nonrequired Reading of 2003*, edited by Eggers and Zadie Smith, who determined that LeRoy was the ideal writer for a student she met "who wore badly chipped black nail polish and a lip ring, had perfect manners, and ended any disagreement or confusion with the sentence 'Well, I'm from Tennes*see*.'" Albert had convinced many people, it's worth bearing in mind, if only to gauge how stunning and brazen her fraud was, that the penis bone from a raccoon serves as a good-luck charm and sexual amulet in parts of the United States. According to Peter Murphy, the pop culture journalist, "LeRoy's Appalachia is a country . . . where people still believe in the talismanic power of a raccoon penis bone." LeRoy regaled another interviewer, for Versus Press, with tales of how he had been known to harvest the bones from roadkill, going on to describe a family whose "life calling" it is "to collect road kill penis bones off coons." British reporters were particularly susceptible to the mythology of the bone. A journalist for *The Observer* helpfully enlightened his readers, "The raccoon penis is a reminder of his hustler times at truck stops across southern America—the pendant is a sexual talisman in the southern states." Another, writing for *The Independent*, noticed LeRoy's habit of nervously fingering his bone necklace as he spoke. "Southern Fried truck-stop hookers" wear such jewelry, the reporter explained, and LeRoy carried his everywhere, "as a potent reminder of his past." In a note to translators that appears on LeRoy's Web site, the author further dilates upon the prized bone:

It can be worn as a necklace or gamblers will wrap a $20 bill around it, tie it with red thread and keep it in their pockets for improved fortunes. Folks will sometimes put a raccoon penis bone beneath the bed or between the boxspring and mattress so that the man or lady with a strap-on will perform better, longer, stronger and harder.

In LeRoy's glory days, such folksy grit and worldly authenticity could be had for a price. Indeed, for $15, or about the cost of one of LeRoy's books in paperback, Albert retailed raccoon bones strung on leather lanyards to all devoted fans and true believers.

LeRoy became well known because of his battered and bruised bio. His writing, such as it sloppily and mawkishly was, was inseparable from the life everyone knew he'd led. When LeRoy was interviewed, as was inevitable, on National Public Radio's *Fresh Air*, Terry Gross mined his life, extracting plangent moments and pathos. Such is her specialty.

Gross: You said you had seen like the adults around you turning tricks, and they made money, and you liked the way they looked, so you wanted to do it too. Were you also exposed to the other side, the dangerous side, the abusive side, the really kind of depressing and dangerous side?

LeRoy: Well, I saw my mom hooking up with guys that used to be abusive. She was very attracted to that kind of personality, and if they were too nice she wouldn't stick around with them much long.

Gross's curiosity about the life of a truck-stop prostitute could not be sated. What was it like, she wanted to know, working as a prostitute when LeRoy's mother was herself working as a prostitute? LeRoy allowed that their relationship could at times get "competitive." But who looked after him when he was younger, who cared for him when his mother was "turning tricks"? He had a lot of friends whose mothers worked as prostitutes too, LeRoy said, so all the kids hung out at the truck stop or in the back room of a diner. "So it was like a whole little subculture, a whole little world," Gross said. "Yeah, it is," LeRoy agreed, "and not that many people are kind of aware that it exists."

People took a liking to LeRoy, a liking that often seemed tinged with the condescension of good intentions. One of his early mentors and guardian angels was the novelist Mary Gait-skill, who later told a writer with *Rolling Stone* that LeRoy made her feel "very alive." He was "extraordinarily charis-matic," though Gaitskill realized from the start that he could also be manipulative. "At the time," she recalled, "I was single. Talking to him, I suddenly had a feverish fantasy that I must find someone to marry and get a house and adopt him. He aroused those feelings in everyone. . . ."

LeRoy had a similarly winning way with journalists. When he and his chaperone Speedy, played by none other than Laura Albert, met *New York Times* reporter Warren St. John for lunch, they ordered $150 worth of sushi, all paid for, of course, by the newspaper. Appearances by the author in the flesh were rare and posed obvious risks, but Albert had recruited a friend, the half-sister of her then-boyfriend, to fill the role as she had imagined it. Notorious, according to St. John, "for their ability to get free stuff," the literary wunderkind and his minder ate what they could and took the rest to go. "They left with enough sushi for a party in their hotel room, which I'm sure

they then had," St. John later told interviewer Dennis Loy
Johnson. "At the time, you think to yourself, well, he's a poor
kid, but he's probably enjoying it. Probably didn't have a lot of
sushi growing up in truck stops in West Virginia."

LeRoy, if anything, sought such pity, drinking up every
drop. When he spoke, he stumbled over tough words, struggling to pronounce them. On the DVD of *My Own Private
Idaho*, for which he contributed an essay and was invited to
provide expert commentary, discussing the film in relation to
his own private experience of life on the streets, LeRoy fum-
bled his way over "literally," "literarily," and "fetishization." He
apologized at one point, saying, "I don't have spell correct on
my vocals, that's what I need." He also reached out to magazine editors and fellow writers, asking for their help, because,
he said, his grammar wasn't so good. Ordinarily, such an admission might be reason enough to have nothing whatsoever
to do with a writer, but knowing what LeRoy had supposedly
been through, many of his correspondents made allowances
and took him under their wide wings. Always his life came before his work. It was like a preface or an editor's note: read this
book, the note said, in effect, but read it in light of my life.

In 2007, a movie production company that had purchased
the rights to *Sarah*, LeRoy's first novel, published when the author would have been all of nineteen, sued Albert. The
company's lawyer argued that the contract was void because
LeRoy didn't exist. "The whole autobiographical backstory
aura that made this so attractive was a sham," he told the jury.
It was, it seems, that backstory they wanted, as much or perhaps more than the novel. The director linked to the project
had thought to combine the book with LeRoy's biography,

creating a film about, according to the lawyer, "how art could emerge from a ruined childhood." While Albert's defense attorney countered that the contract was for a book, not the far richer, more deeply imagined backstory, one can forgive the movie company executives for their confusion. The jury deliberated briefly and determined that Albert had committed fraud, awarding the film company $116,500. A judge later ordered Albert to pay the film company an additional $330,000 to cover their legal fees.

Tall Tales and Believers

So the story goes that a giant grizzly bear was killed, shot dead in Alaska by a ranger with the U.S. Forest Service. The bear, which weighed over 1,600 pounds and stood more than twelve feet high at the shoulder and fourteen feet at the top of its head, was the largest grizzly on record anywhere in the world. In an e-mail about the bear that circulated on the Internet, an anonymous writer put the bear's size into helpful and human perspective:

> Think about this—If you are an average size man: You would be level with the bear's belly button when he stood upright, the bear would look you in the eye when it walked on all fours! To give additional perspective, consider that this particular bear, standing on its hind legs, could walk up to an average single story house and look over The roof, or walk up to a two story house and look in the bedroom windows.

With you-are-there details and an unfortunately sic-worthy prose style, the writer also described how the bear charged the hunter from fifty yards away. The hunter "emptied his 7mm Magnum semi-automatic rifle into the bear and it dropped a few feet from him." But the bear was still alive, the author said, so the hunter reloaded his gun and "shot it several times in the head."

Accompanying that e-mail were several gruesome photographs. In the first, the hunter crouches behind the bear. He could hide behind it and not be seen—the bear is that large. Its snout is bloodied, and blood soaks the grass and the scrubby brush around its body. In the second photograph, the hunter grips one of the bear's paws. It's nearly as broad as the hunter's chest. He has to hold it the way a child picks up a glass, with two hands, and even then, he can barely get his fingers around it.

The Fish and Wildlife Commission performed an autopsy on the bear and, by studying the contents of its stomach, determined the animal had "killed at least two humans in the past seventy-two hours." The writer added, "His last meal was the unlucky nature buff in the third picture below," referring to the e-mail's most gruesome attachment. In that photograph, the corpse of a man is lying on the ground, naked save for a tennis shoe, a sock, and a pair of shorts around his ankle. One of his thighs has been eaten away, and bits of stringy gristle dangle from the bone. His other leg is in far worse shape. Above the knee, it's just a gnawed femur barely attached to his pelvis. Below the knee, there's nothing, the rest of his leg is gone. A person dressed in police blue and wearing latex gloves is crouching over the body, and the corpse's arms are folded across his chest, as if for some measure of dignity.

The story of this giant grizzly bear, while scary and, owing to the photographs, rather morbid, turns out to be made up. What wasn't completely fictional was, at the very least, significantly exaggerated, as stories told by hunters and fishermen some-times are. It is true that a hunter did kill a bear in Alaska. The hunter wasn't a park ranger, however, but rather an airman with the U.S. Air Force, out with a friend for deer. And the animal, while larger than average, measured only ten feet and six inches from its nose to its tail, and weighed between 1,000 and 1,200 pounds. The real bear, in other words, didn't break any world records. According to the hunter, the bear didn't charge them either; in fact, as best as he could tell, it may not have even no-ticed them when he and his friend spotted it "flipping over logs looking for salmon." It's also not true that the Alaska Fish and Wildlife Commission refused to permit the hunter to keep the bear for a trophy. As the writer of the e-mail has it, looking ei-ther to score a point against government bureaucracy or to tack a moral to the end of the tale, the bear "will be stuffed and mounted, and placed on display at the Anchorage Airport (to remind tourist's [sic] of the risks involved when in the wild)."

Soon after the bear was killed, in October 2001, the U.S. Forest Service, Alaska Division, began fielding inquiries from the public about the story. According to a 2003 article in the *Anchorage Daily News*, a woman in Louisiana and a pastor in Michigan were among the first people to receive the e-mail. A year later, the forest service was still answering calls from the curious. They published a press release and tried again, with a combination of firmness and good humor, to debunk the leg-end and replace the outrageous fictions, such as those human remains found in the bear's stomach, with far less captivating facts: the bear's stomach actually contained no human remains whatsoever. Almost every day for several years, the forest ser-vice received killer bear–related e-mail from individuals and queries from reporters wanting someone to verify "a giant, record-setting, brown bear that was shot last week by a forest service employee as the bruin charged the employee!" At first, they fielded three or four queries a day, according to Ray Massey, a USDA public affairs specialist based in Juneau, but, by 2007, they averaged just three or four a month. Massey adds, "We could tell when the e-mail was showing up in a certain part of the country or in a new country—we'd get a rash of e-mails and calls from media."

In 2003, the killer bear story gained new life. As Barbara and David Mikkelson reported on snopes.com, their relentlessly thorough compendium of debunked urban legends and corrected misinformation, someone—sources are rarely named or pinned down in the land of Internet hoaxes—attached that third gruesome photograph. And as the story spread, the bear, not surprisingly, also grew in size and fearsomeness. Able initially to look "on the roof" of that hypothetical single-story house, by the time I received the e-mail, in November 2004, the bear was gazing "over the roof" and peeping into second-story bedrooms. The myth persists but never reveals its age, since the e-mail notes that the pictures and story describe events that occurred "last week," in the perpetual near past. More than a year later, in April 2006, my wife received the bear e-mail from a friend in Denver; the myth seemed still to be going strong. The photographs and story were as I remembered them, though some later recipient saw fit to clean up the grammatical problems that bedeviled the earlier version and then enhance the subject line, from the plainly descriptive "Big Bear in Alaska" to the more attention-grabbing "Hunt Alaska with M60s only."

Most recently, the National Geographic Channel tried to debunk the myth once and for all. The hunter, when interviewed for "The Ultimate Bear," an episode of its *Explorer* television program, explained that he had only e-mailed the pictures of himself posing with the bear to some friends. From there, someone concocted the tall tale, and later someone attached that gruesome additional photo. "That's another picture that gets associated with my bear," the hunter said. "It has nothing to do with my bear." The hunter had his bear stuffed and keeps it at home, in his office, where its head and body nearly graze the room's gabled ceiling. Wherever—and however—the man in the gruesome photograph died, it was not in Alaska. A research wildlife biologist for the U.S. Geological Survey's Alaska Science Center was also interviewed for the program. "If you look at the vegetation in there, it's not quite tropical," the scientist said, "but it certainly is not Alaskan." In his opinion, the corpse appears, he said, "to be the victim of a tiger attack from the Indian subcontinent." No one can rightly say whether the tiger was the largest such animal on record.

The bear e-mail came to me after passing into and out of the inboxes of several reporters and editors at Bloomberg News. From there, it spread to a couple of magazine writers living in Canada and then to my friend, an author and photographer living in Syracuse, New York. I believed the e-mail, at least initially. Sure, the writing was less than great, but I supposed the excitement of the experience could have inspired worse. What got me wondering, especially, what fact really beggared my belief, was the bear on display at the airport. As endings go, it was too fitting somehow, too neat. And also a bit implausible.

Wouldn't showcasing a man-eating bear frighten off tourists? And weren't visitors vital to Alaska's economy? I went looking for a news article, something more soberly written. A minute or so of searching on the Internet was all I needed to let the air out of the tale. I told my friend the news and sent him a couple of relevant links. Later in the day, he wrote back, "Thanks for bursting my bubble, pal."

I hadn't wanted to disprove the story. I certainly felt no satisfaction or smugness upon learning it wasn't true. If anything, I too was disappointed. I had wanted to believe, and so I sought some way to restore an element of the incredible and even awe-inspiring to the factual story. The actual bear, however diminished, was still huge. And that photograph of the hunter with the paw, that was real. That was the actual hunter, and the paw of the bear was, in fact, as broad as his chest. Somehow, however, the facts themselves seemed diminished. Was it the fiction alone that created something incredible? Consider that "incredible" is a word we use to describe both that which astonishes us as well as that which invites our doubt. Did all the tale's power derive from the visceral gruesomeness of that one misappropriated photograph? Or did the knowledge that the story wasn't true distract from the power of whatever facts remained?

Out of curiosity, I traced the path the e-mail took to reach me. I worked my way backwards from recipient to recipient. I could never discover who first sent the e-mail—that would be like determining who started spreading a cold. In any case, the forwarded addresses included in my e-mail only went back a few months; the myth was years old by then. I located an insurance agent in Scottsdale, Arizona, who sent the notice to several colleagues in his office, and I wrote to him as well as everyone else who received the e-mail. I wanted to know what fascinated them about the bear, and what led them to forward the tale along to friends, family, and fellow workers.

Steve Featherstone, the friend who sent me the e-mail, had recently returned from an assignment in Alaska. Mark Schatzker and Mike Randolph received the e-mail just before him. Both were magazine writers living in Canada who specialized in writing about the outdoors. Featherstone told me, "That image of the guy holding the bear's paw brought to mind, immediately, the bear that I saw killed, which was much smaller, of course, but a grizzly bear all the same." He added:

> I saw the bear right after it had been killed by the police—I mean, within the hour—it was still warm, and I put my hand on its paw. I was really surprised at how heavy and meaty the paw was. . . . It felt like concrete it was so heavy. So, seeing those pics reminded me of that moment, and having that great story behind it gave my little anecdote a little more—I don't know what to call it—a little more heft or weightiness.

Schatzker compared the tale to news of shark attacks. Both tapped into anxieties about one's mortality and the dread of sudden, inexplicable death. "Perhaps it's something primitive," he wrote, "fear of being attacked by a beast. The chances of dying this way are remote, but you can't help but relive the horror in your own head."

What, then, made the tale believable?

Featherstone said, "It was realistic because I wanted it to be realistic. I had a self-serving interest to believe in that story." He added:

I doubt that my reasons for believing it to be accurate are similar to most people's, but that's the whole point, it seems. That's the effectiveness of this hoax. It's general enough that it can pluck at a wide range of sympathies, or dearly held clichés about Alaska and bears. . . . That story has a lie for everybody.

Randolph thought the hoax would have been "better" if it got readers to believe the completely implausible. After all, as he said, "bears do occasionally kill and eat people."

"When you think about it," Schatzker told me, "it's very easy to fool people. All you have to do is lie about something somewhat believable. For example, I could tell you I broke my leg last week. You would have no reason to think it's false. There were always guys in high school who would do that—lie about something mundane, then pretend they burned you when the truth was revealed."

As Schatzker and I mulled over the tale of the killer bear, we drifted to the question of the unknown hoaxer's motive. "Why would someone fake it?" Schatzker asked me. "Do they get a thrill out of it?"

When I first began to write about fakes, hoaxes, and cons, in 1997, I was most interested in the fakers themselves, these artists of the fraudulent. As an author of a dozen or so satires, I was, I suppose, a faker of a sort. I had submitted mock letters to the editor, opinion columns, and news articles to a business paper. The pieces all seemed so convincing and real that the editors published them as fact. For a while there, I kept alive enough pen names to field a basketball team and still have a deep bench.

That was hardly the beginning of my life in pseudonyms,

though. In my senior year of high school, a friend and I published an underground newspaper, a photocopied thing laid out with a dot-matrix printer, scissors, tape, and glue. We adopted pseudonyms and attacked the outrages of Ronald Reagan and the follies of the student council and Key Club. I reported on Free Enterprise Day: a staged debate, held before the entire student body, between the forces of capitalism and socialism. Both debaters were, it turned out, motivational speakers. The socialist assured us he had just been acting. We left copies of our work in the school's restrooms and distributed others by hand, in secret, like samizdat. We had many faces, my friend and I. We were Son of Walt Whitman, Phineas Gage, General Secord, Neon Maggot, and about two dozen others besides. Even a teacher who contributed, writing to suggest we lighten up a little, employed a nom de plume.

In college, a friend and I announced that the English department was pleased to offer a writing workshop taught by Don DeLillo. The school was small enough that registration for certain classes was quite informal, a matter of swinging by the relevant department's office and just signing one's name to lists posted on the walls. Like many advanced classes, our nonexistent workshop with the author of *White Noise* included certain prerequisites: first, everyone must have read the works of DeLillo and appreciate them. Reading the works of Pynchon was recommended though not required. A couple of students showed interest, and one of our friends accused us of taking advantage of people while they're at their most vulnerable, at the end of the semester, right in the middle of final exams. At lunch one day, the chair of the English department came up to me and said he'd heard DeLillo was going to be teaching a class. Should be a great course, he said.

Years later, I wrote a satirical gossip newsletter called the *Pearl Files* with Amie Barrodale, then an editor at *The Onion*. Together we became Allen Pearl, founder, editor, and subscription manager of the *Files*. Pearl was a small-time Matt Drudge. He wrote about himself in the third person, nursed angry obsessions with various literary lights, and fell prey to his outsized opinion of himself and his blinding mission to be "the Provider of Insiders with Insider Info." Barrodale and I also invented a hapless band of fictional freelancers. One writer always pitched editors ideas about China and the Chinese. Did the editor know that it has long been a tradition in Chinese culture for visitors to bring gifts, such as candy or money in scarlet envelopes, when they call on friends? Another freelancer worked in a hotel and occasionally delivered room service orders to celebrities. A third was encouraged by one editor to continue submitting queries after she proposed writing about a high-end bakery in Park Slope, where the bakers, who do not exist, are determined to create the thinnest cookie in the world.

I found that writing occasionally under another name was oddly, and surprisingly, liberating. It was one thing to pretend to be a character, as one does when writing from a fictional first person point of view. It was another thing entirely, a joyful thing, to become a different author who was himself creating a character. In "By Any Other Name," *New Yorker* editor Ben Greenman, himself no stranger to pseudonyms, writes about his own experiments with fictional identities. Published, appropriately enough, under a pseudonym, Greenman's story describes the strange thrill of inventing a pen name, along with an identity and body to complement it:

> While writing, I have put on forty years and forty pounds. I have developed a stoop. My 20/20 vision has slipped and fallen into a pit of astigmatism. I lick the stamp with Marvin Mittelman's tongue and mail the letter with Marvin Mittelman's hand. Before the envelope is down the gullet of the mailbox, I have begun to turn back into myself—into ordinary fourteen-year-old Jamie Sidarsky.

The first time I ever faked, I was in the fifth grade, or maybe the sixth. My family lived in Houston then, and my brother and I played baseball in the front yard. Somehow we found out that our neighbor worked for the Houston Astros as a talent scout. Maybe our parents told us. One day, I wrote a letter from the talent scout and addressed it to myself. The letter was effusive but formal. The scout, it seemed, had seen me playing baseball with my brother and was, naturally, quite impressed. Because I demonstrated such incredible promise as a player, he asked me to get in touch with him when I was a bit older. I finished the letter and then painstakingly fabricated a stamp and postmark for the envelope. I didn't bother with the charade of mailing it. When I showed it to my brother, three years younger, he believed it. The letter made no mention of my brother's own playing, except to note that he was present, in the background, when I made my dazzling catches and powerful throws. It was a ridiculous forgery. I handwrote it, for starters. I drew the letterhead with felt-tip markers.

Despite my rather close familiarity with faking, I, like Schatzker, wondered why someone would concoct that tale of the killer bear and send it out into the Internet, where presumably to this day a few more unsuspecting readers will receive a bit of gruesome news from the wilds of Alaska. What drives another faker to create an entire fictional life to lead? Why go to such elaborate lengths? Why would a writer submit fictionalized articles as real? Do most fakers believe they'll never be caught? Do they suppose themselves that clever? Such questions do continue to fascinate me. At the same time, however, I've come to see this line of inquiry as fundamentally unanswerable. When the fakers respond to requests for interviews—and they respond seldom—or write personal accounts of their adventures in dissembling, as journalists Stephen Glass and Jayson Blair both have, they usually prove to be unreliable narrators. True, they're relating events they know well—better than anybody, in fact—but they seem so reluctant to reflect on their past and so allergic to questions of why they did it that they manage only to convey what happened in ways that serve and ultimately preserve their selves.

As I wrote and as I read, I became, with every story and every new hoax, more interested in the faked, in those who believed.

Sometimes I am fooled. I can be a believer.

In the fall of 2005, a student at the University of Massachusetts at Dartmouth began telling his professors and fellow students an amazing tale. While working on a research paper about communism for Professor Robert Pontbriand's seminar on fascism and totalitarianism, he went to the school's library and requested, through interlibrary loan, an unabridged copy of *Quotations from Chairman Mao Zedong*. His professor later explained to a reporter, "I tell my students to go to the direct source, and so he asked for the official Peking version of the book." As a result of the student's innocuous request, two agents from the Department of Homeland Security paid him a visit at his parents' home. They brought the book he asked for with them, but didn't let him have it, informing him instead that Mao's Little Red Book, as it's known, is on a watch list and that, because of the significant time the student had spent outside the United States, he himself had become a subject for their further investigation. The student was a history major, a senior, and by all accounts, an exemplary undergraduate—bright, hardworking, and mature, the kind any professor would want in a class.

The student's story percolated through the history department and made its way around campus, becoming something of a local legend. Students told it to other students. Professors shared it with colleagues. Professor Brian Glyn Williams, who teaches a seminar on terrorism, said the student approached him in a coffee shop and asked if he'd heard what had happened. "I'm the student," he explained, "who got visited by Homeland Security." Williams asked him to sit, and the student told his story. He went play-by-play, using what Williams, whom I interviewed by telephone, called "very precise details." Williams added, "It didn't occur to me to really doubt the story, because by this stage I'd heard it from so many people."

On December 16, the *New York Times* reported that President George W. Bush had, in early 2002, authorized the National Security Agency to eavesdrop on Americans without a warrant. The president's decision to allow such wiretapping inside the country without court approval signaled a major and, to many, troubling expansion of the powers of the NSA, an intelligence agency "whose mission," the *Times* explained, "is to spy on communications abroad" and whose methods are so secret that "it has long been nicknamed 'No Such Agency.' "

At the same time, the Bush administration's rationale for invading Iraq appeared increasingly flimsy, if not wholly fabricated. What was baldly and repeatedly stated as fact—that, say, Saddam Hussein's government cooperated and coordinated its efforts with Al Qaeda, and that one of the September 11 hijackers had met with an Iraqi spy—took on the wan, pasty complexion of discredited fictions. Saddam's vast stockpile of weapons of mass destruction were nowhere to be found, leading to the inescapable, if sickening, conclusion that absence of evidence was, in fact, evidence of absence, and pretty damning evidence at that. As a result, the Central Intelligence Agency's faulty reports were called into question. And the administration's attempts to silence and smear its critics became the rich subtext in a federal grand jury investigation into who leaked Valerie Plame's identity to reporters. At the heart of it all was a forged document, one supposedly showing that Iraq had attempted to purchase, in the president's words, "significant quantities of uranium from Africa." It was a fake, and a badly executed one at that. The national tall tale, that story told and retold to us by the president and the vice president and high government officials, was beyond belief.

In New Bedford, Massachusetts, meanwhile, a reporter with the *Standard-Times,* the local newspaper, called Professor Williams to ask his opinion of the NSA's wiretapping. Williams has traveled extensively in Afghanistan, Kazakhstan, Bosnia, and Uzbekistan. He contributes articles to *Terrorism*

Monitor and has spent recent research trips living with a Northern Alliance warlord, interviewing Chechen field commanders, and talking with Taliban prisoners. Over the years, Williams cultivated sources in Afghanistan, but news of the spy program ended his contact with them. "People in Afghanistan, who I was working with, suddenly found out that their phone calls to the States were being monitored," Williams said, "and they froze up." At the end of his half-hour interview with the reporter, Williams casually mentioned Professor Pontbriand and the student who was visited by Homeland Security agents. It was an afterthought. Williams intended it merely as a possible subject the reporter might consider for a later investigation.

The article appeared the next day, on Saturday, December 17. The student and his brush with the Department of Homeland Security were the subject of a long sidebar to front-page articles about wiretapping and the uncertain future of the USA Patriot Act, which was due to expire. Almost at once, the article, called "Agents' Visit Chills UMass Dartmouth Senior," began to circulate on the Internet. A diarist on the political blog Daily Kos, wasting no time, chimed in that morning, at 8:16. Mark701 was disturbed by the report. It was, he wrote, a "move so typical of this administrations [sic] paranoia." In his hurried retelling, representatives of Homeland Security became agents with the Federal Bureau of Investigation, and he added, "Aside from the fact that the FBI apparently has nothing better to do than monitor books borrowed in Massachusetts, I'm not aware of any terrorist attacks perpetrated by communists on US soil." From the computer of Mark701, the story spread to another Web site, Talking Points Memo Cafe, where Cloudy held up the news article as a blatant contradiction to Attorney General Alberto Gonzales's assurance, in a *Washington Post* editorial which appeared that week, that "there have been no verified civil liberties abuses in the four years of the [USA Patriot] Act's existence."

From the blogs, the story spread to newspapers, to the Web sites of print magazines, and to television. Pontbriand and Williams, who were the reporter's only sources for the article, and secondhand ones at that, received phone calls, e-mails, and letters from around the world. Williams had messages from everyone from the American Civil Liberties Union to a producer with Fox News's *Hannity & Colmes*. Journalists and camera crews descended on the campus. "It was an international sensation," Pontbriand told me in a telephone interview. "I was getting calls from a reporter in Beijing, China." Williams said, "People wanted to enroll in my class from other countries even. I had a letter from someone in Norway saying, 'If you want to teach this class on terrorism, I'll come over there and enroll in it.'"

On NBC's the *Today* show, James Carville repeated the student's story with a bit of embellishment. "A college kid was interviewed," he said, "for three hours by Homeland Security because he was writing an assigned paper on the Chinese communist." Carville's contribution, a detail not reported by anyone else, was the length of the interview, now on the record as three hours. A day later, on December 21, the student appeared in Molly Ivins's syndicated column. He was evidence to argue that, as her title had it, "The President Must Not Be Above the Law." The next day, Senator Edward Kennedy, in a *Boston Globe* editorial, told his own chilling, slightly mangled version of the tale of the student who "had gone to the library and asked for the official Chinese version of Mao Tse-tung's Communist Manifesto." Kennedy saved the student for the conclusion of his editorial. Here was a concrete example of an abstract problem, a human face to gesture toward when discussing a misguided policy. "Incredibly," Kennedy wrote, "we are now in an era where reading a controversial book may be evidence of a link to terrorists." If protests against the government's unchecked power to investigate, eavesdrop, and peer into the private lives of its citizenry had a poster child, the student, who was not named in the original article or the avalanche of subsequent coverage, was now it.

I read about the student in *Harper's Weekly*, a brisk, three-paragraph survey that brings by e-mail the previous week's grim tidings, current outrages, and odd scientific discoveries. Sandwiched between news that the Iraqi military had captured Abu Musab al-Zarqawi, believed to be one of the leaders of the insurgency, only to accidentally release him, and the Senate's decision not to extend portions of the USA Patriot Act, I read:

> It was reported that agents from the Department of Homeland Security visited a college student in New Bedford, Massachusetts, soon after he requested a copy of "Mao's Little Red Book" through interlibrary loan—although many librarians felt the story might be a hoax.

I hadn't heard a thing about this student and his fateful trip to the library. In the headlong rush of my amazement—had it come to this already? bookish college students getting paid visits by grave government agents?—I didn't pay much heed to the doubting librarians and that glaring qualification: the story might be a hoax. Instead, I went online and found the article in the *Standard-Times*. I copied the link into an e-mail to my wife and her mother, forwarded messages and clipped articles being the surest way to share indignation. I typed out a subject line: "College student requests Mao's book from library . . ." In the body of the message, I supplied the sound of the second boot falling, adding, "gets visit from Dept. of Homeland Security agents." With news this appalling, the article spoke for itself.

Days passed, and I thought little about the student who made the unforgivable mistake of being too inquisitive, until I received the next issue of *Harper's Weekly* and read that "the student's story was indeed a hoax." I had been fooled, just like that. I had believed what I read and forwarded it along with hardly a pause to think, let alone doubt. But perhaps I had wanted to believe. It had, after all, become all too easy to expect—and accept—the worst from Washington. Being fooled and believing seemed to me then increasingly inter- changeable, even indistinguishable. Belief collaborates with a lie. It smoothes over the lie's rough edges until the lie feels silken. Whatever is implausible, whatever richly deserves the steady gaze of our skepticism, instead hardly merits a raised eyebrow. Readers of fiction are, per Coleridge, said to suspend their disbelief. Yet the converse is also true, though less often stated: people can believe, willingly, in what they know not to be true. Fakers require—and exploit—such willing believers.

For Pontbriand and Williams, getting at the truth became both a personal and professional obligation. Their names were associated as sources, albeit unwitting ones, to a sensational news article. Members of the Association of College and Re- search Libraries were among the first to raise factual questions about the student's version of events. The student had claimed he gave the library his Social Security number, but the library never required that information. Did the student merely misremember, or had his story sprung a leak? Professionally, the story held the long-term potential to make the professors' students anxious about undertaking research. "Here I am trying to teach students to look at Hamas Web sites and read books about Zawahiri and bin Laden," Williams told me in our interview, "and a lot of them are skittish before this." Students routinely asked Williams if they were allowed to look at such Web sites. He had to reassure them that they weren't doing anything anti-American. As a result, Williams worried that the student's story could become "an article of faith" and "a legend that was there forever." He explained:

> People across the country would have known that people who do interlibrary loans expose themselves to investigation. I mean, you have no idea how many students . . . would have digested this view of the world. When you're an educator, that flies in the face of what you're trying to achieve.

As the story spread, the student vanished. E-mails and phone calls to him went unanswered. A few days later, during finals period, Pontbriand spotted the student in the hallway and "dragged him into my office." For the next several hours, he and Williams grilled the student. A university spokesperson showed up, as did the reporter from the *Standard-Times*. They asked him to tell his story again. They asked him questions. They wanted details. Though the pressure on him was great, the student stood by his account. "He was not nervous or sweaty," Pontbriand said. "He even held the reporter's tape recorder in his hand while he told the story."

But still, the professors had their doubts, more than ever.

There were simply too many inconsistencies. "He had great confidence in himself in telling this tall tale, but it was just a tall tale," Pontbriand said. "It was a remarkable story, but it was a lie." That night, Williams sorted through all that they knew and made some phone calls to libraries, inquiring about their interlibrary loan procedures. He worked like a detective, or a good reporter. He called a friend at the Department of Homeland Security to see if they had any agents by the names the student had provided. They did not. Furthermore, as a spokeswomen for the department later pointed out, they don't even employ their own agents. The story was coming undone, and Williams worked at the threads until two in the morning. The next day, he drove to the student's house and confronted him with his suspicions. "After initially trying to stand by his story," Williams said, "he finally recanted it."

What fascinated Williams was how alone he and his colleague were in wanting to separate the few facts from the much more tantalizing fiction that overwhelmed them. "Nobody wanted to get to the truth of the matter for the right reasons," he told me. The story served every political interest, from liberal to conservative. It was a powerful symbol, something concrete and easily grasped that stood in for something larger. What's more, the story encouraged—and supported—self-interested interpretations. To those on the left, the story proved beyond every doubt that the Bush administration had run amok, again. "It reminded you of the McCarthy era at its worst," Williams said. "For the right, it was another case of 'Here's the left assaulting the very nature of the policies we use to protect ourselves.'" The professors received hate mail and congratulations in fairly equal quantities. "People on the right instantly pegged me and Bob as 1960s, ex-stoner, liberal professor types," Williams said. "I was actually born in 1966 and have no memories of Viet Nam." Other readers suspected the professors of concealing a hidden agenda, perhaps even of making the whole story up in order to hurt the president. Once the truth was revealed, though, and the professors proved the student's story a tall tale, the right took a turn singing the professors' praises—how great was it that these scholars only wanted to get at the truth?—and the sharpest criticism then came from the left. According to several feverishly conspiratorial Web sites that Williams read, the truth was elementary: Williams must be employed as a secret agent for the CIA, Pontbriand was in the National Guard, and both were ordered to "hush the whole thing due to government intervention." Case closed, I guess.

But why did so many people, including myself, believe the student's tall tale, ignoring every red flag and tabling their every misgiving? And why do people fall, and fall quite routinely, for such fakes? In *The Counterfeiters: An Historical Comedy*, Hugh Kenner writes, "We are deep, these days, in the counterfeit, and have long since had to forego easy criteria for what is 'real.'" In this 1968 study of reality and artifice, Kenner considers satirists and forgers, wondering if one can be told apart from the other. He examines comedy and gravity, parody and soulless imitation. He writes about being human, on the one hand, and automatons and early robots faking human behavior, on the other. He addresses a rich and teeming variety of subjects in *The Counterfeiters*, subjects which, he readily admits, "the Dewey Decimal system . . . prefers to keep in different parts of the building." In the mid-1950s, he first noticed that comedians were ridiculing President Dwight Eisenhower not through mimicry of his speech or stilted movements, those fail-safe techniques of the working comic, but by getting on stage and reading—simply reading—transcripts of his official remarks. Kennedy-era comedians followed suit. What was real was funny, or at least could be when put in another context. Kenner sensed something new afoot.

Another commentator on the frequently trespassed border-land between the real and the fake observes, "We have a hunger for something like authenticity, but we are easily satis-fied by an ersatz facsimile." That was written by English pro-fessor Miles Orvell in 1989—not English novelist George Orwell, as repeated citations on the Internet would have one believe. (It does seem appropriate somehow to find a falsely at-tributed quote about fakes floating around the Web.) In *The Real Thing: Imitation and Authenticity in American Culture, 1880–1940*, Orvell measures how far the fake has encroached on the real. While his state-of-the-fake survey mostly con-cerns the years fenced in by the subtitle, Orvell does examine the contemporary age in his introduction and epilogue, where he covers one dead-on example and unmistakable truth after another, from Wild West–themed eateries whose walls are caked with "cowboy artifacts" to an officially designated spot in Grand Canyon National Park where visitors are directed for "guaranteed . . . excellent snapshots" to the docudrama *Roots*, which boldly celebrates an indifference to representations of reality when its voice-over declares, "There you have it . . . some of it fact, and some of it fiction, but all of it true, in the true meaning of the word."

These real-seeming fabrications are still very much upon us. According to Orvell, Americans not only tolerate such ersatz facsimiles with "grudging good humor," they love the fraudulent stuff. Orvell's diagnosis here is, I'm afraid, a bit cheery. We actually hate the fake and soundly reject it, or at least we try to whenever we realize we're in its presence. Yes, we may now accept the utterly false in theme restaurants and we may be reticent before the seemingly inevitable appearance of yet another build-your-own Irish pub, but we don't much tolerate undisclosed fiction mixing in with our facts. Imitation we can condone, but not invention. Imitation flatters and may even entertain, but invention and, with it, deception never sit well. We scold the fakers, the authors, the disgraced journalists, all those who conned us with their clever inventions. And yet, however much we may loathe the dastardly hucksters, we are still taken in by the considerable charms of their many fake things. We are simply fake's fools.

In September 2006, London's *Guardian* newspaper landed an interview with James Frey. It was the author's first since he appeared on Oprah Winfrey's television show that January and attempted, haltingly and awkwardly, to defend his own sense that, sure, some of what he wrote may have been invented or embellished or otherwise made up but all of it was still true, in a way. Since then, Frey's publisher had amended his book to include an apologetic letter from the author to his readers. "*A Million Little Pieces*," Frey wrote, "is about my memories of my time in a drug and alcohol treatment center." His is a book, in other words, not about a period in his life, but about "his memories" of that period. He wrote it, as slippery witnesses who come before congressional committees are wont to say, to the best of his recollection. Still, apology or no, dissatisfied readers brought a class-action lawsuit. Those whose expectations of the memoir genre were not quite as capacious and forgiving as Frey's own and who demanded more than memories and what the author had taken to calling, at various points, the "subjective truth" of his "manipulated text," turned in page 163 of their hardbacks (or the front cover of their paperbacks) and received, in return, refunds from Frey and his publisher. So Frey was, to say the least, a bit wary. He brought his own tape recorder with him to the interview.

As it turned out, he had little cause for worry. The reporter sought to place Frey's misdeeds—and the widespread uproar that greeted them—into some larger, more useful context, namely a world of fakers more prominent than he. "A man who is known to have manipulated the story of his own past is allowed to occupy the White House," she pointed out. Also, it seemed readers now possessed an enlarged appetite for facts. "Our recent desire for facts," the reporter wrote, "is an indication that we are recoiling from a culture that has grown increasingly synthetic." Perhaps so. Frey, for his part, was only too happy to point his finger somewhere other than at his own chest. "I think a lot of it had to do with what was happening and is still happening in our country, y'know?" he told the reporter, apparently meaning the war in Iraq, among other things. "People feel frustrated by a lot of distortions by politicians, by members of the media, by movie stars, by tabloid journalists, and it was like a sorta confluence of events that I happened to be in the middle of." Grasping for other possible explanations for the furor his book stirred up, Frey mentioned the fact that the United States is "a puritan society" and "a young culture, with . . . less of an artistic and literary canon than some of the older European cultures."

Quite right, although another, less tenuous reason might be that people don't much like to be fooled. In general.

We are living in the season of the fake. From Frey and his fake tales of drug-addled dissolution to the author formerly known as JT LeRoy and his fake rural tough-talk and fake tales of decadence to Stephen Glass and his fake dispatches from the fringes of religion, politics, and culture, we are beset by real-seeming fiction masquerading as truth. More recently, in 2008, Margaret B. Jones, the half–Native American, half-white author of *Love and Consequences,* a critically lauded memoir about gang life in South Central Los Angeles, was revealed to be one Margaret Seltzer, a white woman who grew up on the mean streets of Sherman Oaks, California. Seltzer attended a private Episcopal day school that counts Mary-Kate and Ashley Olsen among its alums and currently costs more than $25,000 a year. Like Laura Albert before her, Seltzer was a pity artist. She dreamed of drug dealing and gangbanging and so invented a new life for herself, a new name, a new persona, even a nonexistent foundation, called International Brother/SisterHood, created, its Web site claimed, to reduce gang violence. Seltzer sought sympathy from her readers. She was the stray dog begging to be taken in from the storm, the baby abandoned on the doorstep. In exchange she offered her supposedly hard-fought wisdom, her treacle, and her tears. As Chris Lehmann, who wrote about *Love and Consequences* for *The Nation,* observed, the memoir industry is guided by two lodestars: "extremity in suffering and the quiet grace of self-deliverance." Once a gang member, now a survivor, Seltzer brought the grit and the redemption, the tough tales flecked with her streetwise authenticity and the personal knowledge found through her recovery. "Time," she told a publicist who interviewed her for a Q&A appearing on the publisher's Web site, "heals all wounds but you still have the scars."

The *New York Times* lavished the memoir with a "Books of the Times" review by Michiko Kakutani and, two days later, puffed the author in an extended profile for the "House & Home" section. National Public Radio's *Tell Me More* was planning to include host Michel Martin's conversation with Seltzer in a series on gang life. For the interview, which NPR posted on its Web site after the ruse was exposed, Martin and the author discussed possible scenes she could read on the air. In one passage, the author and her younger sisters are walking home from the grocery store when one sister, Nishia, drops a carton of milk. Recounting the same incident in the publisher's Q&A, Seltzer said:

> It burst open and the milk streamed into the gutter. She burst into tears, begging me not to be mad as she stooped down trying to scrape it all back into the broken carton. I told her I wasn't mad. But I was. That was a half-gallon of milk wasted and two dollars gone. Even now, as an adult, just thinking about that—thinking about the choices you were given as a child that weren't kid choices—makes me want to cry.

So many tears, over so much literal spilled milk. Seltzer cried each time she read that scene and so, she said, did her editor. After the interview, Martin told the author, "I just wish I could hug you, that's all I wish I could do. . . . I wish I could protect that five-year-old."

How much of what seems real is now fabricated, designed expressly to scare or elicit sympathy or amaze and delight, before simply melting into air? What, or who, can we trust? In the wake of Frey's and LeRoy's deceptions, the *New Yorker*, tapping into the climate of uncertainty, published a cartoon in which a student stands beside his teacher's desk and confesses, "Mrs. Briner? Remember all that stuff I said I did on my summer vacation? I didn't."

Our fakers are believed—and, at least for a time, celebrated— because they each promise us, screen-gazing and experience-starved, something real and authentic, a view, however fleeting, of a great thing rarely glimpsed. *Hermenaut* editor Joshua Glenn explored this efflorescence of the falsely real, suggesting that "whenever 'authenticity' is evoked, we are already in the world of fake authenticity." Here, we are assured, is the memoir of a troubled addict who found success after suffering through hell and then rehabilitation. Here are heart-rending short stories, produced by a young writer who once was troubled, misunderstood, and abused but has now found success and made many celebrity friends. Here are true tales of a tough life, as only a survivor can tell them. Here are the pictures of a hunter who stood before a killer bear and brought the beast down with his gun. Here is something real.

Yet here is also where the unending, and quite possibly futile, quest for authenticity gets rather complicated. For the authentic tales we crave most are typically removed from our own experience. We read about people quite different from us, and that distance makes it difficult for us to judge when we receive something real, which we very much want, and when we're slipped yet another real-seeming fake, which tricks us. Nan Talese, the publisher of *A Million Little Pieces*, shared her way of knowing with Oprah Winfrey, when she appeared on *Oprah* in Frey's defense:

> Now, the responsibility, as far as I am concerned, is: does it strike me as valid? Does it strike me as authentic? I mean, I'm sent things all the time and I think they're not real. I don't think they're authentic. I don't think they're good. I don't believe them. In this instance, I absolutely believed what I read.

But believability (what we think is true) gets confused here with authenticity (what is true). And thus, good writing gets confused with authentic experience. A memoir, like Frey's, may be a good, quick read without being wholly authentic. In fact, what's considered good about it, or believable, and what draws readers in, may distract them from ever asking if it's real. What's more, the book's authenticity could be a quality not of the raw experience described but of the writing being read. We may describe a novel as baroque or a narrator as deceitful, observations made about the writing itself. Do we mean anything more when we claim a memoirist's account seemed authentic? As Winfrey said, "One of the reasons why we're all so taken with the book is because it feels and reads so sensationally that you can't believe that all of this happened to one person." Except of course, one *can* believe it all happened to one person, and many people clearly did believe, as Winfrey and Talese both can attest.

Does authenticity arise then out of our miasmic feelings,

from some vague gnawing in our guts that we may or may not trust? Say a person wants to read about a West Virginia–born male prostitute and his gang of street urchin friends. That reader has no real ability to judge whether that life, as written, is authentic. The story seems real, but maybe the story just reads well—smoothly, classically—and those qualities entertain us momentarily. But what, finally, does the reader know about what is real? Chances are, he doesn't have any friends from West Virginia. Maybe his university's football team played there once, but he didn't go to the game. Come to think of it, he's never even driven through the state. So far as he knows, maybe young male prostitutes do form informal gangs. And perhaps they do keep childish pets like snails and frogs as their talismans against a world that treats them cruelly. Who is the reader, finally, to doubt another's experience? Our culture of therapy and self-help, which gained considerable steam in 1969 with the publication of *I'm Okay, You're Okay*, has, in the years since, inspired the seemingly endless parade of novels and memoirs about addiction and recovery, abuse and survival, a parade in which Frey and LeRoy march at the front. And yet, the very principles of therapy bind our language and restrict as much as aid our ways of communicating with one another. Consider how therapy counsels that one's experiences, like one's feelings, are untouchable, above both reproach and judgment. Experiences, when presented in memoirs or, in the case of LeRoy, as autobiographical and confessional fiction, can't be easily, or comfortably, questioned. One may, of course, like or dislike such stories, but it's thought inappropriate, or perhaps even a form of psychological violence, to inquire if the stories truly happened as the author claims. In a *Los Angeles Times* editorial published in the wake of the Seltzer imbroglio, media critic Tim Rutten argued that "the only unchallenged moral authority has become that of victims . . . only those who have experienced pain or torment have a right speak of it, though others may participate vicariously through their eyes."

We many, we voyeuristic many, we want the real, and indeed we hunger for it, but we also want our real stuff to be engaging and entertaining and come in readily consumable packages. In an essay about the scandals that buffeted the media in the late 1990s—from Glass's fakery to Patricia Smith's invention of characters for her columns in the *Boston Globe* to Mike Barnicle's joke-lifting and character-creation for columns published in the same newspaper to CNN's report, later proven false, that U.S. forces in Vietnam dropped sarin, the lethal nerve gas prohibited under international law, on civilians as well as American soldiers suspected of being deserters—Lewis Lapham argued that journalism lacked the golden age for which its critics often wish. "The volunteer critics apparently choose to forget," Lapham wrote in *Harper's*, "that before Rupert Murdoch and Larry King, there was William Randolph Hearst, that before Jenny Jones, there was Henry Luce." To Lapham, all journalism, regardless of its vintage, was simply storytelling, and some stories possessed more beauty, complication, and truth than others. "All stories move from truth to fact," Lapham writes, "not the other way around, and in their endeavor to convey the essence of the thing the tellers of tales must give it a name and age and address." He adds, "People like to listen to stories, to settle into the wilderness of their experience with the fence posts of a beginning, a middle, and an end."

Otto Friedrich, Lapham's editor at the *Saturday Evening*

Post, came to understand the high value assigned to narrative while working, in the early 1950s, for the United Press, in its Paris bureau. While France fought for lost causes in the colonial uprisings of Algeria and Vietnam, Friedrich and his fellow reporters stayed well clear of both conflicts, the better to keep the cost of news-gathering to a minimum. Instead, the writers were charged with taking bland press releases from the French government—so many insurgents killed, the terrorists on the run now—and transforming them into dramatic news articles. But editors found Friedrich's work wanting. "I was," Friedrich recalls, "soon taken aside by the assistant bureau chief and scolded about what he called 'your all-the-news-that's-fit-to-print approach.' " Friedrich, a fine writer whose essay collection *The Grave of Alice B. Toklas* is regrettably out of print, was told the job required some attention to facts, but also a great deal of enthusiasm. Merely factual stories, ones that reported what happened, were likely to be spiked. In time, Friedrich learned to stop worrying and love enthusiasm. "What is 'enthusiasm'?" he asks in his essay "How to Be a War Correspondent."

> It consists of writing about something as though it were exciting, even though you know nothing about it, even though you are thousands of miles away, even though it is not exciting at all. The basic technique involves verbs of action, lots of adjectives, a sure grasp of clichés, and a readiness to fill in gaps where the facts are missing.

When the Agence France-Presse ticker alerted the bureau that planes had just bombed the communists, the enthusiastic reporter wrote, "Waves of American-built Bearcat fighter-bombers zoomed low over cleverly camouflaged Red positions and rained down bombs and fiery napalm. . . ." In an enthusiastic story, Friedrich writes, soldiers "never 'go' anywhere; they 'slog through waist-deep rice paddies,' they 'wade through turbulent flood-swollen streams,' or they 'knife through sweltering jungles.' "

Those values, storytelling's values, meet the art of faking in "The Hoaxer," a piece of short fiction by Walter Kirn, about a father and his reluctant son who fabricate supernatural occurrences for others to discover. They start with simple crop circles and work their way up to "Howling Johnny, the mummified wolfboy of Glacier National Park," the father's most daring fake. The father assembles Johnny from an old skeleton and clumps of his own hair, and gives him some primitive-looking musical instruments made out of elk gut, antlers, and the like. "People won't *want* to explain this thing," the father says. "It's magical."

Johnny descends from much earlier hokum, such as the bits of skull and a jawbone dug up in southern England, in 1912, in a discovery that came to be called Piltdown Man. Scientists of the day believed Piltdown Man to be a missing evolutionary link, albeit one that confounded their theories. Indeed, they took more than forty years to debunk the archaeological hoax. Piltdown Man was preceded in the annals of fakery by the Cardiff Giant, a petrified man measuring ten feet from head to toe who was found in central New York, in 1869. If Piltdown Man was a cagey imitation, meant to deceive, the Cardiff Giant was plainly wicked satire. The man who fashioned the hoax was a tobacco dealer and, not incidentally, an atheist who had quarreled with a minister about whether the Bible could really be accepted as literal truth. The minister maintained that every word was true. The Book of Genesis spoke of giants because, the minister said, in the beginning of the world giants did stride across the land. QED. The atheist wanted revenge. He buried the giant on his land, waited a year to exhume it—he was nothing if not patient—and then, while installing a well, he pretended to make his great find. The giant proved a popular—and profitable—tourist attraction. P.T. Barnum tried to buy the giant; when his offer was refused, he just made himself a copy and declared the original a crude impostor. Archaeologists, it must be said, were not fooled—the stone giant bore visible chisel marks—but some men of faith did greet the discovery as tangible proof of their religious convictions.

For proof, the father places into Johnny's rucksack a yellowed newspaper clipping referring to a real boy, long since disappeared. Even the most impossible fakes may be held together by a thin tissue of tiny facts. The old article rounds off their creation and extends a helping hand to assist any archaeologist who might stumble upon what they made and feel at a loss for an interpretation. When the son wants to bury Johnny hastily and just leave him already, his father, speaking for all accomplished fakers, advises him to take more care. "It has to be near the snow line. Off the trail more," he says. "Also, we need a cliff he could have fallen from. It has to make a story."

Frey too wanted to make of his life a story. In his apologia, he says of his own writing, "I wanted the stories in the book to ebb and flow, to have dramatic arcs, to have the tension that all great stories require." Therein lies the problem, and the writer's predicament, for life does not often, if ever, resemble literature's great stories. Life is an unedited mess. Life is so many spools of raw videotape, a long and winding transcript preserving every "uh," "um," and "oh." Life, were it like a movie, painfully lacks dramatic arcs. Much of it, to be fair, is simply not dramatic. Instead, life is sparked by an arbitrary beginning and then interrupted by an unpredictable end. It proceeds in fits and starts and consists of quite a few slow patches. Stories, however, promise the rigorous and ruthless adaptation of lives, shaped in accordance with the high demands made by meaning, consciousness, and style. Frey added, almost predictably, "I altered events and details all the way through the book." How could he not? One would almost have to doctor life, bending and even breaking it in places, if arcs and drama were key aims.

Frey's stories, while not great, do have the virtue of coming in easily digested forms. They're sleek and rounded, like pills. They don't much tax the busy reader. If anything, they encourage— and abet—a kind of narrative tourism, whereby a reader can journey to a dangerous or exotic place but need not linger long. Reading about the recovered drug addict or reading the fiction of a former male prostitute makes considerably fewer demands (on one's time, energy, and self) than, say, volunteering to work with people in need of help, people with real stories, crazy stories, stories which probably don't make half as much sense as Frey's and LeRoy's, stories that are not, sorry, classically told, with satisfying dramatic arcs punctuated by either wry, ultimately comforting ironies or tight-lipped frowns, to indicate deep reserves of personal strength in the face of immense sadness. We like such stories, but we also want the lives we read about to be artfully expressed by expert narrators. But can we really have it both ways? The desire for authenticity and a welltold story, for gritty dispatches from little-glimpsed lives unlike our own and a yarn as traditional in its design as a fairy tale, will forever be at odds. Such a combination is, at the very least, exceedingly rare, like an ancient artifact believed lost, or a priceless work of art thought destroyed. What's more, our desires invite the creation of fictions that seem real, or are at least real enough to be convincing, but which ultimately offer only approximations of the genuine. Consider the buying and selling of art and antiquities: whenever a market exists for the exceptional and the uncommon, forgers rush in, viewing it as an opportunity to fake and counterfeit.

Fakers, by their nature, remain elusive. They seek not to be discovered. They leave no fingerprints. Their signature is invisible or looks identical to another person's. The most gifted fakers will themselves to vanish, leaving behind only the work they made: the forged painting, say, which we nonetheless admire, or the seemingly true story, which engages and entertains us no matter how incredible it seems or how false it's proved to be. "The counterfeiter's real purpose," Kenner writes, "is to efface himself, like the Flaubertian artist, so that we will draw the conclusion he wants us to draw about how his artifact came into existence." Believers too are elusive—though for far different reasons. They may be embarrassed or feel disinclined to relive the moment they were taken in by a faker. "When did you first realize you were fooled?" is a question nobody looks forward to answering, but for years now I have worked under the assumption that the question is in fact worth asking, and asking anew, and that the answers can tell us much about what we believe and what we want, why we trust and why we still get duped.

A Story Born Every Minute

Stephen Glass is infamous for the wrong reasons. Media critics, professors of journalism, and his fellow reporters have pored over the published work of the former writer for the *New Republic*, who, in 1998, was fired for fabricating some or all of twenty-seven articles. Such scrutiny would appear justified if the writing in question was, say, the sonnets of Shakespeare or the overlooked novels of some forgotten Nobel Prize winner. After all, only a tiny portion of history's first draft can bear the attention of even a second reading in the evening, after work. Yet in the rush to understand how and why Glass fooled so many people so many times, his professional readers have lavished their critical interest on thin fictional fare like "Hack Heaven," about a petulant fifteen-year-old computer hacker holding a software corporation over a barrel, and "Peddling Poppy," about the First Church of George Herbert Walker Christ, a group of evangelical Christians who wander from city to city testifying to their belief that the former president is "descended directly from the Messiah." Perhaps no one's journalism has received as close a reading as Glass's. But while Glass's critics may read closely, most misunderstand wildly and choose to view his rise and subsequent downfall as a tragedy or, as *Washington Post* media critic Howard Kurtz described it, "a cautionary tale." Kurtz and others derive from Glass's performance (brilliant, but flawed) and its various reenactments—the feature articles in *Vanity Fair* and elsewhere, an autobiographical novel by Glass, and a movie about him—a series of object lessons and tidy morals. By making a strident show of dismissing Glass, an individual who dared to break their rules, they comfort themselves and fortify their profession, but leave unquestioned the fundamentals of journalism.

Glass's article about the hacker did him in, finally. An editor at the Web site for *Forbes* magazine upbraided one of his reporters for letting a staid, inside-the-Beltway magazine scoop them on a hot story about the software industry, so the reporter started asking questions. When he couldn't locate a single source Glass used, when the phone number for this "big-time software firm" in California turned out to be a cell phone in Delaware registered to Glass's brother, and when nothing else checked out, the *Forbes* reporter contacted the *New Republic* and asked them to explain.

Glass's exposure inspired a great deal of melodramatic soul-searching among media folk. Writing in the *Boston Globe*, Tom Rosenstiel, director of the Project for Excellence in Journalism, laid out a high-minded, four-step manifesto and called for newspapers, magazines, and television news bureaus to preserve the "historic standards of journalism" by returning to the values that made the profession great:

Step 3: A news organization must make these values clear to the audience—in effect, making a covenant with the public about what it stands for. This covenant is critical. It is the only way for the audience to fairly judge what it thinks of a news organization. It is also the only way for journalistic values to matter to the bottom line.

The *Houston Chronicle* went back even farther, to the very basics, writing, "There is one question that people in the news business should never have to wrestle with. It is never OK to report falsehood and fiction as fact." Even *USA Today* got in on the action, glumly editorializing: "The wreckage of journalistic integrity continues apace. . . . The compact [between readers and the media] lies in tatters nationally." The *American Journalism Review* looked for and eventually located a silver lining, albeit a small one: "The press is being held more accountable. By the press." Hairshirts worn two sizes too tight were the height of summer fashion that year among writers and editors along the Eastern seaboard. This was due, in part, to the sheer flagrance of Glass's fabrications and what everyone saw in hindsight as the outrageousness of his inventions. See, for example, the Monicondom, a prophylactic specially designed for oral sex and poised to capitalize on what Glass called an exploding industry in memorabilia inspired by Monica Lewinsky's and President Clinton's gettings-on. But the media's excoriation of itself was due also to the fact that Glass was not some obscure freelancer struggling on the fringes of magazine writing; he was one of them, and up until the discovery of his serial fabrications, he had been their darling, publishing prominent features in *Rolling Stone*, *Harper's*, and *George*— remember *George*?—all of which proved later to be fiction to some extent. When Glass was fired, articles by him were set to run in upcoming issues of *Mother Jones* and the *New York Times Magazine*; editors at both magazines did a little more fact-checking and decided it best to kill the features. Because Glass got around, editors and writers had good reason to want to make sure there was enough crow for all.

Glass was a brilliant storyteller, or so his story goes. His articles burst with the sort of feverish, anxious invention that sometimes can seem like life. A typical Glass story focused on a colorful, eccentric character. In one fabricated article, the director of a public-interest organization dedicated to good nutrition dissected his sweet-and-sour chicken with an absurd "surgico-priestly air" as Glass sat interviewing him. Glass delivered snappy dialogue, too, always managing to capture that brand of speech in which the subject has no clue what an ass he's making of himself. There is, for example, the bond trader who worships Alan Greenspan, asking the chairman of the Federal Reserve for guidance on bullish days—"When things go well, I hold the Greenspan picture between my two hands and say 'thank you' "—or bearish ones—"When things go poorly, I also take the photo in my hands and pray." A Glass article is chockablock with quirky and comic details. At the National Memorabilia Convention, a fictional event, a vendor hawked a computer game where the object is to guide Lewinsky from her apartment in the Watergate Hotel to the Oval Office. A few booths down, another vendor is selling the new inflatable sex doll that recites racy bits from Walt Whitman's *Leaves of Grass*. Glass also had the luck to witness dramatic scenes as they were unfolding. In one declared fake, Democratic staffers file down into the basement of a house for the secret unveiling—at midnight, naturally—of their homemade "Newt-O-Meter," a device that tabulates the amount of money the former Speaker of the House owes for his ethical violations. Elsewhere in the naked city, young Republicans, wasted and restless, hatch schemes to find an ugly woman and really, like, humiliate her, all in the presence of the intrepid reporter. When Glass was working at the height of his powers, he included all of these elements in one economical lead paragraph.

Jack Shafer, writing for *Slate* shortly after Glass was fired from the *New Republic*, explained what he felt made Glass's writing so special and singular, so Glassian. He turned in "stories with energy and imagination and originality," Shafer said.

> The filigree of detail dazzles. Some of his better pieces read like textbook examples of New Journalism, fusing the world of fact with the literary power of narrative. He doesn't just write about teenage hackers, he tracks a pimply member of the species down to his Bethesda home where a software company is signing him to a contract. He interviews the adoring mom.

Leaving aside the question of whether it's really that great an accomplishment, when writing about an adolescent, to go the extra mile and interview the adolescent's mother, Shafer identifies the wrong source of Glass's uniqueness. What Shafer misses is that Glass's wild inventions form a thin skin stretched over a fairly standard body of accepted truth and mainstream opinion. Glass's imagination is not, in other words, all that original. It is, in fact, crushingly banal. How else to explain his production of so many fabrications that deliver, in story after story, the shared assumptions of the editorial class in new and perhaps slightly surprising forms?

That bond trader and his buddies, however quirky their habits (another is busy testing a handheld urinal so he won't ever have to get up from his desk and miss an important phone call), all serve to illustrate just one central and comparatively drab point, a point that Glass and his coauthor for that article, Jonathan Chait, felt bore repeating, over and over: Alan Greenspan is a powerful man who makes important decisions that affect the economy, and as a consequence, people treat him with the deference shown a god walking among mortals. This point is not news. It is not original or imaginative. It does not actually dazzle. It is, instead, a given. It is a common assumption, and it reads, in its simplicity and naïveté, like the thesis statement for an eighth-grade social studies report. Proposed thus to an editor, that editor would pass on the article without a second thought. But were the point, widely assumed to be true, found embodied in the behavior and antics of a group of bond traders, and then brought to life in a well-appointed corporate setting, with the reporter promising he can gain rare access to the palace of the privileged, that same editor might express some interest.

One editor who did, repeatedly, was Richard Blow at *George*, who published two of Glass's made-expressly-to-order articles and bought a third. In each case, Glass delivered the story exactly as Blow desired it. When the editor wanted an article about how celebrities aid the passage of legislation, Glass found what Blow calls, in his 2003 *Salon* confessional, "the money shot statistic": an invented political consultant who had studied that very question and determined, preposterously, that legislation with celebrities attached "was ten times more likely to be voted into law than that which wasn't." How, incidentally, would such a study even be conducted? By experimentally submitting pairs of identical bills to Congress, one with a juicy celebrity endorsement and one without? During the Lewinsky scandal, Blow was anxious, he said, "to dig up some dirt" on Clinton friend Vernon Jordan. Glass obliged his wishes, concocting stories from women who confided that Jordan was a "boorish lech" and inventing anonymous quotes from the lawyer's colleagues, thus providing fly-on-the-wall coverage of the imbroglio and a fleeting if obvious glimpse of Jordan nervously pacing his office underneath the watchful gaze of his own portrait. Blow declares that a "great image," but is it really? And even if it were true, what does it contribute to what we know? A slight sensation and a shiver from spying Jordan in his natural habitat? Glass's talent lay less in the originality of his imagination than in his solicitous ability to seize on whatever the conventionally wise were chatting about at cocktail parties and repackage it in bright new containers, selling the palaver right back to them. Nobody was the wiser. "To really understand why the story of Steve Glass still causes such pain," Blow writes, "you have to know that making up facts was only part of what Glass did to his colleagues." He adds, "We opened ourselves to him, and in turn he probed our minds, pinpointing our vulnerabilities, our vanities, our prejudices. He exploited the worst in us and betrayed the best."

With the publication, in 2003, of Glass's novel *The Fabulist* his flair for animating stereotypes, letting clichés inhabit human bodies, and ordering characters to stand in for lazy ideological assumptions became more evident. His novel tells the story of a reporter named Stephen Glass, who works at *Washington*

Weekly, a contentious and feisty magazine of politics and opinion not so much based on the *New Republic* as carefully traced
and then colored in a bit more garishly. Glass, only occasionally roused to something reminiscent of satire, sends up some
of the real magazine's counterintuitive cover articles, inventing
two all-too-plausible ones: "Clinton: Our Most Moral President" and "The Case for Being Out of Shape." Glass the character, like Glass the author, fabricates a story, gets caught, has a
lot of explaining to do, tries to lie his way out of the jam, falls
apart, and then is fired. "Glass" discloses how his life was in
shambles and how journalists tormented and stalked his every
movement. "Glass" instantly despises journalists once he can
no longer count himself among them. "Glass" details how he
found enlightenment in a lap dance and, later, learned a little
something about himself during a trip to a massage parlor with
his brother. In no time "Glass" gets his life back to together,
finds a job as an assistant manager at a video store—the real
Glass graduated from Georgetown Law school and was offered an appointment to a prestigious clerkship—then redis-
covers God, and, of course, falls in love. "Glass," unlike Glass,
also explains himself. Where the author had, before the publication of his book, never granted an interview, his character
tells his side of the story.

That story reads, in part, like one long, not-terribly-
productive therapy session and, in other parts, like the script to
a cancelled sitcom. All the parts are rife with clichéd language.
Of a girlfriend, Glass writes that "her pixie blond hair and
gamine charm go straight to my heart: I can't believe how for-
tunate I am to be with her." Situations in the novel end predictably. When "Glass" and she of the pixie locks travel to
Savannah, Georgia, for a Valentine's Day date, they visit

Johnny Mercer's grave, and "Glass" is inspired to sing her the only song by Mercer he knows. When he's done, his girlfriend looks at him "lovingly," runs her hand through his hair, and then asks him "to promise never, ever to sing to her again." This is sitcom timing, the way a gag rushes sentimentality off the stage, and no characters will let tenderness linger between them for longer than a couple of beats. It's no surprise but nonetheless dismaying when characters compare what befalls them in the book's climactic scene to something on *ER* and then, when their predicament worsens, to a horror movie. "Glass" meanwhile reflects on how his life seems increasingly like a television show.

However small the screen of his life, for "Glass" self-discovery is the only order of the day. His father mails him an article about his fabrications, written by an older journalist who got his start in journalism by working the police beat for a small newspaper. The older journalist believes what "Glass" did is indicative of a younger generation of journalists, a careless lot and blindly ambitious. When he finishes the article— "Glass" calls it a screed—he says, "I agreed with a lot of it, but I resisted even thinking anything so critical of journalism: it felt too much like kicking the victim. Whatever larger lessons might be drawn from my predicament, I wanted to concentrate on the small ones: the lessons I hoped could someday help me make a new life."

All this concentration—a more accurate but less gentle word for it might be "indulgence"—paid to his inner life does take its toll on the lives of other people in the novel and the world they inhabit. It is Glass's world, finally, and they're stuck in it until the end. One of Glass's explanations for fabricating characters and stories is that he wanted the world to appear as he imagined it. "I was describing the world, I knew even then, as I wished it to be," he writes, "not as it was." His impulse here is an idealistic one, perhaps even utopian, but what's troubling is how, exactly, Glass and "Glass" apparently wish the world to be.

The worlds described in the novel and Glass's collected fabrications are cartoons, in which people's emotions, thoughts, and convictions are governed by strict rules inherited from movies and television programs. His characters' lives seem ideally put to a soundtrack of singsong music (for happy times) and raspberry sounds (for sad ones). "Glass" gets embroiled in all sorts of madcap hijinks and hilarity—situations that would not be out of place in any televised life—including but not limited to dressing like the woman whose voice he's trying to fake in order to get into character, wearing his girlfriend's underwear so as not to wake her by getting his own, wearing a garbage bag when his girlfriend's underwear rips, and going swimming with a group of mahjongg-playing elderly women while wearing—no, not the garbage bag—a Speedo owned by a woman's deceased husband. Late in the book, "Glass" loses his job at the video store (he's fired for being honest, for doing the right thing—so touching), and feels angry as he drives home because the weather is sunny and bright. "All I could think was, Why can't it rain? It's supposed to rain at times like this," he writes.

> In the movies, in books, on TV, in Shakespeare's plays the weather replicates the content of the story—but not now. The sun, the goddamn luminous sun, beamed down on me in all my misery.

How ironic.

• • •

The people in Glass's journalism fare no better. The pickiness of the man with the sweet-and-sour chicken is meant (not subtly) to undermine his political beliefs and make his lifelong goals for clearer nutritional information on food and a public better educated about their diets look as silly as his obsessive and bizarre table manners. In another article, Glass introduces us to a man who thinks Successories, the company that prints those dreadful posters with "Teamwork" showing a crew team rowing down a river and "Quality" showing a lone jogger, is in part responsible for his business's growth and his personal well-being. The man cannot merely think this, however, as untenable as it is. No, in Glass's world he must take his belief to absurd lengths, and Glass obliges with descriptions of how "his eyelids drop halfway, almost as if in prayer," and how his "lips curl into a slight, beatific smile." In another article, at a conference to discuss Ronald Reagan's legacy, two academics hold opposing views regarding the president's support for aid to the Nicaraguan Contras. Their beliefs and differences—which are not, tellingly, represented in the article—draw them "into a shoving match in the cafeteria, knocking over trays of food." A woman in Chicago who supports the budget-balancing ideas of Paul Tsongas and Warren Rudman and the rest of the Concord Coalition displays a large portrait of Tsongas ("the messianic man with the wise, sorrowful eyes, eyes that look deep into your sinning soul") on the wall of her home.

These are all cartoons of belief, and Glass treats his believers—any activist, really, or marginal subculture—like dupes, made to look foolish for the mere fact of their disagreement and opposition. What's more, Glass uses marginal groups—his articles are riddled with fictional NGOs and not-for-profit organizations—to confirm the continued validity of his assumptions: the resistance remains small, the powerful face no real challenges. Glass condescends to this minority of believers as if they were a primitive tribe, there for him to study and display, squatting in the mud, superstitiously rubbing their idols and mumbling their useless and unintelligible magic words as the real business of politics marches on without them.

After the discovery of Glass's misdeeds, various critics pointed their fingers at Glass and the *New Republic*, seeking answers to the question—the perennial question whenever such scandals occur—*Why did he do it?* Glass was an over-achiever, critics said. His parents had not thought journalism a worthy pursuit for their son and hounded him to do better. Others said the *New Republic*'s editors were too young. Its writers were inexperienced and promoted too quickly. Its fact-checking department was too small, part-time, and overtaxed by the publication of a weekly magazine. Glass, they said, had helped reform that very department, thus possessing the necessary inside information on how best to deceive them.

None of the explanations washed, really. Each suggested an easy fix or quick remedy. Just hire more fact-checkers and have them work full-time. What could be easier? Editors too young and inexperienced? Well, get older and more experienced ones and, please, whatever you do, keep the young ones on a shorter leash. Problem solved. Now let's get back to doing what we've always done best: reporting the truth. The explainers had this wonderful knack for leaving the institution of journalism standing in favor of making an example of the profession's most public offender.

Fake journalism, however, didn't begin and end with Glass.

Before Glass, speaking only of recent memory, there was Janet Cooke at the *Washington Post*, winner of a Pulitzer Prize in 1981 for a moving article about an eight-year-old heroin addict who did not exist. After Glass, Patricia Smith and her colleague Mike Barnicle, both of the *Boston Globe*, were forced to resign for turning in fiction. CNN and *Time*, discovering the joys of corporate synergy and collaboration, retracted the story they reported about the U.S. military using sarin gas in Laos during the Vietnam War when the allegation proved false. And that was just in 1998. Later years saw the publication of fabricated journalism by Jay Forman at *Slate*, Rodney Rothman at the *New Yorker*, Michael Finkel at the *New York Times Magazine*, and Jayson Blair at the *New York Times*. After Glass, the pattern simply continued: journalists did wrong, editors were lax, and the profession circled its wagons against the newest and latest malicious individual.

Even repairs made to the *New Republic*'s editorial ship, however significant, somehow did not manage to put an end to fake journalism. In 2007, the magazine published three diarist pieces, brief first-person accounts from a pseudonymous soldier stationed in Iraq. The stories were grim and, at times, flippant. An affectless been-there-shot-that quality was punctuated only by sharp blasts of black humor. The writer—U.S. Army Private Scott Thomas Beauchamp, as was later revealed—told of a fellow soldier who found a piece of a human skull with clumps of hair still attached and wore it like a crown, marching around and squealing to everyone's apparent delight. Elsewhere, the writer and his buddy publicly humiliated a woman—perhaps a soldier, perhaps a civilian contractor, they're not sure—who had been disfigured by an explosion, her face severely scarred, her skin melted. The duo was eating in a crowded DFAC, the mess hall of our present war, when the woman entered and sat near them. "I think she's fucking hot," the writer said. He blurted it out loudly enough for everyone to hear, and then regaled his friend with his idea for a pin-up calendar called IED Babes. The woman ran out, and his buddy just laughed and laughed. Another private entertained himself by taunting wild dogs into the streets of Baghdad and then running them over with his Bradley Fighting Vehicle. Under fire from conservative commentators and bloggers, who questioned both the facts as well as what they considered an unbecoming portrayal of U.S. soldiers, the editors at the *New Republic* undertook to verify the articles more rigorously than they had. Five months later, editor Franklin Foer reported what some readers had already assumed: too many questions remained either unanswered or unanswerable. What's more, many of Beauchamp's stories could only be confirmed as anecdotes that other soldiers too had heard but none had seen firsthand. The magazine lacked confidence in Beauchamp's version of events, Foer wrote. They would no longer stand by his stories.

Fictional journalism is essentially a careful imitation of journalistic forms. That is, the articles are convincing because they adhere closely to the unstated conventions, assumptions, and predilections of a particular publication, a particular kind of article, or a particular editor. Journalists who fake are extraordinarily sensitive to the ways in which their stories are a series of sometimes conventional, often routine forms. Most journalists, however, see the form of their articles as transparent, a clear vehicle for transmitting the truth of what happened—the facts—without affecting, altering, or in any way coloring it. Their form conveys the story but does not change it. This belief rests on a tremendous naïveté, or a willed ignorance, about writing and language. Fabricated journalism can tell us plenty about journalism as it's practiced today—if, that is, anyone cares to consider it as something more than aberrant, the shoddy work of isolated individuals who just don't share the profession's values. News stories considered great, funny, heartrending, or dramatic that turn out to be fake make real journalism—the reporting done by people who play according to the rules—appear, at the very least, suspect. But fabricated journalism also raises questions about how the profession prizes, and gives prizes to, stories that feature great characters and dramatic leads, literary qualities which may not be, strictly speaking, incompatible with reporting the truth, but which may, at the same time, encourage some reporters to shade that truth a bit here and there.

Such journalistic fabrications should best be considered the way art historians and museum curators approach fake works of art. Forgeries, they believe, unwittingly reveal the taste and temper of their times. They disclose what seemed authentic. They tell us what once was taken for real. In recent years museums have published catalogs and mounted entire exhibitions of faked art. They're not celebrating their fakes or glorying in being duped; they're studying the forgeries and putting them into useful contexts in order, say, to understand the art market of the time or to discern a forger's source of inspiration. Agnes Mongan, a curator and, later, the director of Harvard's Fogg Art Museum, once purchased a delicate Matisse drawing called *A Lady with Flowers and Pomegranates*, which was later shown to be the work of Elmyr de Hory, a forger so deft that he sought to follow up the deal by dashing off a Renoir and a pair of Modiglianis, offering to sell them to the Fogg as well. This was in 1955. In time, Mongan came to appreciate fakes and even urged the museum to collect them. She realized they could serve an important pedagogical purpose by helping students learn better to detect them.

I saw for myself how fakes give up their creators, exposing them, while looking into the odd, conflicted career of Louis Marcy. Marcy was an antiquities dealer who sold forged medieval and Renaissance objets d'art. Based primarily in London and busy faking between 1890 and 1930, Marcy offered art collectors everything from swords and knives to drinking cups and caskets. He successfully placed his fake wares in the Metropolitan Museum of Art, the British Museum, and the South Kensington Museum (which became the Victoria and Albert Museum). J. Pierpont Morgan bought several pieces and became Marcy's patron. While most forgers cultivate intense and narrow specialties, Marcy and his workshop trafficked in works made from copper, gold, iron, and silver, as well as amber, ivory, leather, and wood. Some fakes were cleverly made to appear broken, aged, or incomplete, according to Marian Campbell and Claude Blair, curators at the Victoria and Albert who are cataloging Marcy's fakes. A medieval chessboard made of oak, which would be quite rare were it not a fake, was made to seem pocked with wormholes. Marcy was also an anarchist who published his own magazine—a short-lived zine, really—called *Le Connaisseur*, which he wrote largely by himself. From the pages of *Le Connaisseur*, Marcy ranted indignantly about the art world, excoriating collectors and curators for their bottomless desires so easily sated by fakes—his, of course, among them.

At the Metropolitan Museum, I got the chance to peruse their Marcy holdings, which include one of a very few complete runs of his magazine. To examine today a medieval horn from the Marcy workshop is to be struck, first, by how different their sense of the period was from our own. His fakes appear almost baroque, so heavy are they with decoration and elaborate ornaments. The horn—made, like all Marcy's fakes, in the long shadow of gothic revival architecture—rests on a metal pedestal and is flanked by a miniature castle and tower. An angel nearly as tall as the castle stands atop the horn with a staff in his hands. I found it hard to understand how such a piece, a gift from Morgan to the museum, ever passed as plausible, let alone how it was accepted as real. Were people more gullible then or more trusting? Did they have fewer opportunities to view genuine objects of the period?

The answer has more to do with how fakes lose their power to fool. The effective lifespan of a forgery, Mongan often said, is but a single generation. We're not likely, in other words, to get fooled by the fakes of our fathers. Looking at forgeries much later, a person schooled in different aesthetic traditions and comfortable with other visual languages can see them for what they are, noting, say, the forger's overly fancy, even fussy line, which, in the case of Mongan's fake Matisse, bears the mark not of the modern master but something more conspicuous and contemporary, a more than passing resemblance perhaps to certain elegantly drawn department-store advertisements from the 1950s.

Journalism's fakes, these exquisite examples of well-executed forms, are no less revealing. The content—those hackers, the worshipful bond traders, the heroin addict, and all the fiction that's secreted away inside—seeks first to satisfy the formal requirements; that is, the professional expectations and limitations journalists work under every day. Yet there are articles—real articles, these, about true subjects—that cannot be easily written or are not practical to publish simply because they don't fit one of the accepted forms. Those accepted forms doubtless make certain stories easier to tell and more likely to be repeated, while stories that don't so easily fit a form—that don't, say, have a dramatic narrative shape or lively characters who say wild, unpredictable things—don't get written and published. At the very least, these forms create limitations that bend and warp the stories that reporters do write. Journalists and editors may, in the face of such scandals, drum the offenders out of their midst, then publish critical articles about themselves, and even form august committees to study how best to preserve the profession's values, but making an example of Stephen Glass and the other fakers, as much as they deserve it, won't fix what's wrong. The exercises in self-flagellation, while certainly loud, will remain shows only, fervent displays of conviction and resolve, until journalists and editors look at Glass and the other fakers not as anomalies from their own, better selves, but as fellow journalists still, people whose work cannot be separated from what they do every day. What journalists need to accept, finally, is that what the fakers do is tell stories, and telling stories has always been fundamental to what reporters write and how they write it. Telling stories to readers, in fact, may be journalism's oldest value, preceding by centuries the guarantees of truth, objectivity, and "All the news that's fit to print."

Paper Moon

On August 21, 1835, close readers of the *New York Sun* may have noticed a terse announcement tucked away on page two regarding "astronomical discoveries of the most wonderful description." John Herschel, a British astronomer working at the Cape of Good Hope in South Africa, was responsible for these new breakthroughs and was assisted in his endeavor by "an immense telescope of an entirely new principle." The announcement—a single sentence really—was reprinted, as was the lazy custom then, from another publication, in this case the *Edinburgh Courant*. It ended there, without a specific word for what the discoveries were exactly.

Four days later, on August 25, the *Sun* made good on its tease, delivering the first of several lengthy extracts purportedly from the *Edinburgh Journal of Science* and written by an assistant to Herschel lucky enough to have witnessed the exciting discoveries. What followed was a lumpy blend of rhetorical throat-clearing, technical details about the power of

Herschel's telescope, invocations of the Creator and His "mysterious works," and a good bit of promotion and self-congratulation.

The article began a bit dryly, particularly for the *Sun*, which had, since its founding less than two years earlier, made local crime stories its specialty. If it bled, it led at the *Sun*, where the news was conveyed, for a penny a day, with a flippant smirk. The *Sun* prided itself on giving its working-class readers colorful tales from the streets and not the sort of daily updates on the government that they were sure to find (but unable to afford) in the more respectable, better established six-cent papers.

But for this occasion, if on no other, the *Sun* republished news from the world outside lower Manhattan. "We have the happiness of making known . . . to the whole civilized world," it said, "recent discoveries . . . which will build an imperishable monument to the age in which we live, and confer upon the present generation . . . a proud distinction through all future time." While all this sounded not unlike a tiresome introduction to a far more interesting keynote speaker, the gist of Herschel's discoveries was, at long last, made plain: Herschel had "obtained a distinct view of objects in the moon, fully equal to that which the unaided eye commands of terrestrial objects at the distance of a hundred yards" and "affirmatively settled the question whether this satellite be inhabited, and by what order of beings." In other, fewer words: Herschel had discovered life on the moon. He had seen it with his telescope. In the supplements to come, readers could expect "engravings of lunar animals." Other pictures, the paper promised, would follow.

The publication of this newspaper series even today is remembered as one of this country's most elaborate hoaxes. The lone fact that helped substantiate the more outrageous passages was that Herschel was a real astronomer of popular renown who came from a family of famous astronomers—his father was the first to observe and name Uranus. The hoax was meant to be a satire, or so at least its real author, a newspaper reporter employed by the *Sun* who concocted the real-seeming fictions with the blessing of his editor, later claimed. The object of that satire was overheated scientific prose and editors of competing newspapers. But the articles were also a colorful by-product of the circulation wars that papers then fought as they tried to woo advertisers and attract readers, resorting to any means possible, stooping even to hoaxes when honest reporting and objectivity failed to work. The *Sun*'s moon hoax illustrates both the gullibility of American audiences, which is well known now, and the cynicism of journalists and editors, which was well known even then. The hoax also reveals what many people, in 1835, believed. What seemed to them true or, at least, possible and even likely? What did they assume, however naïvely, that science and technology might one day achieve?

New Yorkers lived on an island that was already, by spurts of growth and periods of rapid development, filling up and slowly expanding to the north, above Canal Street—today the generally accepted dividing line between upper and lower Manhattan, but the city's northernmost street through the 1820s. Even as late as 1849, the city stopped at 14th Street, leaving the rest of the island untransformed—its dense forest, a few scattered farms, and the temporary camps of those who couldn't afford housing, all yet to be turned into regular city blocks. With life unfolding in plain view of such drastic and daily changes, was it really inconceivable that a scientist would spy miraculous creatures on the surface of the moon?

Richard Adams Locke didn't believe so. Locke, who was born and educated in Britain, had founded the London *Republican*, a newspaper that failed for the obvious political reasons, and then the *Cornucopia*, a magazine that folded when readers didn't warm to its mix of literature and science. In 1832, he moved to New York and quickly found ample work as a writer. Locke became highly sought after by editors and well paid, in part because most other reporters then were by trade printers first and writers second, if at all. Locke worked for a penny paper that competed with the *Sun* and was covering the sensational murder trial—no murder trial lacked sensation to a writer for a penny paper—of Robert Matthias, a.k.a. Matthias the Prophet, a self-made religious leader who killed one of his followers and then claimed first to be Jesus and then God himself. The *Sun*'s publisher asked Locke to write for his paper, too, on the side, and Locke agreed. In a few months he went from writing about a fake prophet in White Plains, New York, to becoming the *Sun*'s head writer, to fabricating a fake vision of the moon.

The *Sun* didn't typically publish articles on important national and world affairs. Its motto was "It Shines for All," which sounded optimistic enough and may even have been true, but the *Sun* did not illuminate all. It didn't cover partisan politics. It didn't feature long, intelligent treatments of public affairs. When Iowa and Wisconsin were admitted to the Union, the newspaper devoted three lines to the news. In *The Story of the Sun*, published in 1918, Frank O'Brien explains the newspaper's editorial vision:

It must not be thought, however, that the *Sun* did not attempt to treat the serious matters of the day. It handled them very well, considering the lack of facilities. The war crisis with France, happily dispelled; the amazing project of the Erie Railroad to build a line as far west as Chautauqua County, New York . . . the ambitions of Daniel Webster; and the approach of Halley's comet—all these had their half column or so.

This was not a publication that strived, in the best tradition, to comfort the afflicted and afflict the comfortable. The *Sun* just did its best to entertain. Still, it filled a void, shedding some light on a New York that ordinary New Yorkers experienced firsthand. At the beginning of the nineteenth century, most newspapers were specialized publications, tailored primarily to merchants who depended on the announcement of ship arrivals and their cargoes as well as information on trade and commodity prices. Most of these papers could claim fewer than two thousand subscribers. But by 1830, just before the dawn of the *Sun*, forty-seven newspapers were published in New York, eleven of them dailies. The more than 270,000 people who resided in New York in 1835 enjoyed extraordinary media diversity. They could read trade papers, abolitionist papers, newspapers affiliated with political parties, a Catholic paper and an anti-Catholic paper, immigrant papers, a labor paper, and business sheets, among many others. *Freedom's Journal*, an African American newspaper, began publishing in 1837.

Into this noisy, competitive market entered the *Sun* and its rivals, the other penny papers. Each was an upstart, and every one busily tried to win readers over with lively, sometimes slang-filled writing, an intriguing headline, or a story nobody else had told. According to Frank Luther Mott, whose indispensable history of American journalism remains unequaled more than forty years after its first publication, the penny papers owed their success to new technology—namely, faster, more efficient steam-driven printing presses. John Tebbel, another historian of journalism, argues that an economic depression in 1833 made the new penny papers a gamble but ultimately did nothing to slow their success. If anything, owners of the *Sun* and its competitors benefited handsomely from the larger number of readers who couldn't afford the more expensive publications. It was the papers' writing, however, that made them truly popular, steering clear of both high-toned political editorializing and the sort of dry data featured in the mercantile newspapers and finding instead a voice equal to the energy and enthusiasm apparent in the fast growing city of New York.

The *Sun* splashed its stunning report of life on the moon across the news page, but the editors treated the scoop as if their readers would be in no great rush to get to it, letting them dive instead into a bewildering, almost interminable description of Herschel's second telescope (the first had cracked): how it was constructed, what, exactly, it was made of, and how it differed from his father's, which he had inherited. The article made time also for leisurely forays into such arcane subjects as the history of telescopes, the history of astronomy, and the universe as it was then known. It's hard to imagine Locke, the unsigned mastermind behind the hoax, establishing the credibility and authenticity of his science fiction any more slowly. He wanted to entertain readers, sure—just very slowly. His moon hoax moves at such a glacial pace—and the writing is so apparently sound and sober—that readers of the day likely found it difficult to recognize they were being teased at all, let alone completely had. And so, in that first dispatch, on August 25, Locke stuck to the seemingly factual, disclosing for example that Herschel's telescope measured twenty-four feet across. It weighed "nearly seven tons after being polished" and had a magnifying power of 42,000 times—enough, according to the article, to reveal "objects in our lunar satellite of little more than eighteen inches in diameter." Further details about any actual lunar discoveries remained few, until the following morning's edition and its breaking news.

With the second dispatch about moon life, the *Sun* had acquired quite a following among readers, overwhelming its team of newsboys and taxing its printing presses. The *Sun* took "scrupulous care" to correct its earlier report, explaining that the Herschel telescope had in fact cost £70,000 and not $70,000, observes Ormond Seavey, a George Washington University English professor, in his 1975 introduction to a reprint of Locke's moon hoax. Herschel and his assistants panned that considerably pricier telescope across the surface of the moon. What they saw was breathtaking, a wilderness idyll. A broad, level green plain gave way to a deep forest with trees unlike any they had seen, except, one assistant suggested, "the largest kind of yews in the English churchyards." One discovery followed closely on the heels of another. The narrator—Locke's moon hoax is written as if a junior scientist and member of Herschel's team had recorded the group's observations for the benefit of the scientific community—was ecstatic. "Then appeared as fine a forest of firs," he said, "unequivocal firs, as I have ever seen cherished in the bosom of my native mountains."

Not all the moon's flora was so familiar. Herschel, according to Locke's hoax, discovered a long chain, stretching thirty to forty miles, of slender, obelisk-shaped pyramids the color of lilacs. His assistants thought them architectural, the bold monuments of a new race of people, but the senior scientist, soberly and quite reasonably, pronounced them "quartz formations," no doubt of the "wine-colored amethyst species." The formations measured between sixty and ninety feet tall. None of the scientists had ever seen such crystals, but they kept their heads, took notes, and made observations, sticking as best they could to the scientific method. Locke, who studied science as an amateur, permits his narrator a few controlled lyrical exhortations, but always steadies those more emotional, highly charged moments with sturdier, more even-keeled passages informed by reason, logic, and scholarship.

On a lunar beach, while Herschel and his team watched, a "strange amphibious creature," perfectly spherical in shape, rolled into and out of the telescope's frame. Not far away, in "a perfect zone of woods" surrounding a quiet valley more than twenty miles wide, "small collections of trees, of every imaginable kind, were scattered about the whole of the luxuriant area." Herschel's assistant, and Locke's narrator, was breathless and excited. He added, "Our magnifiers blest our panting hopes with specimens of conscious existence." The scientists discovered bison there, in that "perfect zone." They resembled the bison on Earth, except were slightly smaller and had a "fleshy appendage over the eyes." Locke has his fictional Herschel hypothesize that the cap must protect the lunar bison from "the extremes of light and darkness." It stood to reason; other creatures, after all, were similarly outfitted. Not far away, in the same valley, a blue goat ran and sprang about like "a young lamb or kitten." In these goats, the scientists derived "the most exquisite amusement," watching them appear on their screen—the telescope supposedly projected all these wonderful discoveries onto a large screen, much like a movie projector, which wouldn't be invented for almost another sixty years. Scientists played at catching the image of a particularly agile goat, "attempting to put our fingers upon its beard," only to see it "bound away into oblivion, as if conscious of our earthly impertinence."

Even more extraordinary details followed in the third part Locke wrote, published the next day, and readers in greater numbers flocked to the paper to read that latest report. They found stories of volcanoes, and glimpses of more bison, a larger species it seemed, red and white birds taking wing, long-tailed birds assumed to be like golden and blue pheasants, moose, elk, a small reindeer, a horned bear, and a petite zebra, about three feet high, "which was always in small herds on the green sward of the hills." Herschel and his team identified thirty-eight new species of trees and nine mammals in all, including a sophisti- cated beaver that walked upright, "carri[ed] its young in its arms like a human being," and lived in primitive but well- constructed huts. "From the appearance of smoke in nearly all of them," said the *Sun* dispatch, "there is no doubt of [the beaver's] being acquainted with the use of fire."

With the publication of the fourth, most sensational in- stallment, on August 28, the *Sun* became the largest circula- tion periodical in the world. Regular subscribers in New York City numbered 15,440. With sales in Brooklyn, out-of-town orders, and purchases direct from the boys who hawked the freshly printed fabrications in the street, the total came to 19,360 readers. The *Times* of London, by comparison, sold 17,000 copies. In order to satisfy demand for the moon story, the *Sun*'s presses ran for ten hours a day. People wishing to purchase a copy hung around outside the offices until three in the afternoon, on the mere rumor of a later reprint edition. Those who could get their hands on a copy of the new excerpt read about the greatest discovery of all: human beings on the moon. No journalist before or since Locke has ever buried a lede so deep.

The creatures, who averaged four feet in height and had yellow faces and shocks of copper-colored hair on their heads, flew with the aid of long, thin, almost translucent wings, which they could fold neatly behind them. The scientists likened their wings to those of bats, and named the Lunarians *Vespertilio-homo*, Latin for man-bat. The man-bats' "attitude in walking," the Herschel team reported, "was both erect and dignified." They lived in pastoral bliss, spending "their happy hours in collecting various fruits in the woods, in eating, flying, bathing, and loitering about on the summits of precipices."

Locke lavished many words on the happiness of his fictional creations, from the beauty of the man-bats, which "appeared in our eyes scarcely less lovely than the general representations of angels by the more imaginative schools of painters," to their ability to live without apparent strife: "The universal state of amity among all classes of lunar creatures, and the apparent absence of every carnivorous or ferocious species, gave us the most refined pleasure, and doubly endeared to us this lovely nocturnal companion of our larger, but less favored world."

On the moon, the valleys were always lovely and green, and

the hills, mountains, and promontories were so often described as beautiful—sometimes snow-white marble, sometimes semi-transparent crystal—that Locke apologized for "the poverty of *our* geographical nomenclature" and reflected on the difficulty of portraying them in what words he had, writing, "However monotonous in my descriptions, [they] are of paradisiacal beauty and fertility, and like primitive Eden in the bliss of their inhabitants."

At a time when the United States was fast becoming more industrialized and crowded and its citizenry increasingly and bitterly divided by the question of slavery, it can be no accident that the *Sun*'s postcards from the moon became such objects of fascination. From a branching river filled with slow-moving water birds to thick veins of gold visible on the surface of the moon, there for the easy taking, to hills topped by such intense yellow and orange crystals that the scientists supposed them on fire, every paragraph opens its own idyll and provides further evidence of a happy, flourishing pastoral society. Locke's fabrication was elaborate, true, but it was also wishful.

New Yorkers had good reason to show a weakness for tales of such an Eden. Social stresses of every sort—between blacks and whites; Protestants and Catholics; immigrants and the Europeans who styled themselves natives; gang leaders, whose members took control of the streets in June 1835, and the elected officials who depended on them for help in getting out the vote; bosses, a relatively new word, from the Dutch, and their laborers—all led to regular and often bloody confrontations. Social inequality increased each year, as the standard of living for many declined. Most people in the city rented, and most renters endured close quarters, diseases, and squalor, note

Edwin Burrows and Mike Wallace, authors of *Gotham*, the magisterial history of early New York. Coal stoves, gas lights, and iceboxes were available, insofar as they existed, but remained priced out of reach of all but the wealthiest citizens. For the rest, oil lamps and candles were the order of the day, along with regular trips uptown into the woods to scavenge for decent firewood.

The roads were either crudely cobbled or unpaved, and traffic was unregulated, a free-for-all. Pigs ran through the streets, let out to root for food or eat trash. In a rare show of concern about sanitary conditions, city officials corralled the hogs, enraging their owners and touching off a conflict that boiled and cooled several times over the course of two years, leading eventually to widespread rioting—a prologue to the tragic anti-abolitionist riots of 1833 (which won just the usual half column in the *Sun*). Davy Crockett, not anyone's idea of an urban sophisticate, visited New York for the first time and published a ghostwritten account of his unpleasant trip the same year Locke's fantasy took hold. "I do think I saw more drunk folks, men and women, that day, than I ever saw before," Crockett, wrote of one impoverished, working-class neighborhood on which the *Sun* depended for readers. According to Luc Sante, the author of *Low Life*, a history of the city's seamy side in the years between 1840 and 1919, which he describes as its "adolescence and early adulthood," Crockett also saw people, whom he characterized as "worse than savages," filling the streets. They burned the straw from their beds. Their cellars were "jam full of people." Crockett quickly had enough. He turned to his guide and said, "God deliver me from such constituents, or from a party supported by such."

Little wonder that, in the face of such grim living conditions, New Yorkers developed a taste for escapist literary fare like James Fenimore Cooper's romantic sagas and Washington Irving's satirical history of New York, a book that presented the young, shallow city with a deep, vibrant, nearly mythical cultural history to call its own. Locke merely had the bright idea to relocate Eden to outer space. Yes, his moon hoax was a complete fantasy, but it masqueraded as fact and relied on details that were all too easy to believe. On Earth, the numbers of bison and beavers dwindled, decimated by the fur trade. On Locke's moon, the animals thrived. Readers, their sensibilities softened by romanticism even as their lives coarsened, growing more naturalistic, believed such details simply because many might well have wished they still held true of their world.

Locke's story was read widely and reprinted as quickly as the new pages could be set in type. The *Sun* published a special pamphlet edition, which compiled the separate installments and retailed for an unheard-of thirteen cents, and sold all sixty thousand copies printed in less than a month. Herschel's breakthroughs were debated heatedly and evaluated by a contingent of scientists from Yale University (they believed the published account). The articles were praised—said the *New Yorker*, no relation to the magazine of Eustace Tilley, "The promulgation of these discoveries creates a new era in astronomy and science generally"—and damned, with hardly a paper passing up the chance to reprint some of the articles themselves. One rival paper even published a parody.

Then on August 31, the *Journal of Commerce* unmasked Locke as the author and declared his work a fraud. Other papers echoed the charges, but the hoax could not be finished off so readily. Newspapers of the day denounced one another as a matter of routine, often just for the sake of competition and the public attention that loud denunciations inevitably earned. Locke responded to the charges, rebutting them in a letter first printed in the pages of another newspaper. He insisted "as unequivocally as the words can express it, that I did *not* make those discoveries"—but did so disingenuously, as a way to fan the flames. To the *Sun* any criticism of the moon hoax merely extended its life. The *Sun* welcomed any and all harsh words about its work, even going so far as to reprint them, thus finding a way to magically transform all the bad press into publicity and increased circulation.

In mid-September, after several weeks of back and forth among the city's papers, the *Sun* broke its own silence about the hoax in order to suggest, not very helpfully, that the story had a "useful effect in diverting the public mind, for a while, from that bitter apple of discord, the abolition of slavery." In a way, the editors couldn't have been any more honest. The moon hoax had been an entertaining diversion indeed, though not a welcome one, necessarily, and not just from slavery. New Yorkers had any number of bitter apples to chew on. Their apartments were in shambles and the streets ran thick with sewage. Internecine social tensions simmered angrily, like grease in an iron frying pan, then exploded into full-on riots. Locke only came along and enticed them with candy.

Though the *Sun* had willingly sacrificed any chance for a reputation built on accuracy, it continued to grow. In December 1835, the paper reported on the devastating fire that tore through Wall Street and burned twenty blocks, sending up flames that were visible in Philadelphia. Almost seven hundred buildings were destroyed, and early estimates suggested the cost of rebuilding would be at least $20 million. An English paper in China reprinted the *Sun*'s article—in the aftermath of the moon hoax and the wake of its infamy, the newspaper's articles were read the world over—but counseled its readers not to get drawn into another trick. By August 1836, one year after Locke's first word about Herschel's wonderful discoveries, the *Sun* was publishing 27,000 copies every day, 5,600 more papers than the daily print runs of all eleven of the city's six-cent papers put together.

While the *Sun* came in for periodic drubbing, if not open disdain, both during and after the hoax, Locke was not without his fans. P.T. Barnum, himself no stranger to hoaxes, declared Locke's work "the most stupendous scientific imposition upon the public that the generation with which we are numbered has known."

Edgar Allan Poe was another famous admirer, though slightly more grudging in his praise. Three weeks before Locke's first article appeared, Poe had published the first part of his story "The Unparalleled Adventure of One Hans Pfaall" in the *Southern Literary Messenger*. In the story, Pfaall builds a ship and travels to the moon in order to escape his considerable financial debts on Earth, a plot development no doubt inspired by the impoverished writer's own wishful thinking. Poe intended to continue the tale with at least one more part, detailing Pfaall's landing on the moon and relating what he found there. Once Locke's articles began to appear, however, Poe abandoned the story. Poe felt sure that Locke had read his work (Locke said he hadn't) and stolen the idea (the stories are not that similar in their detail or design). Over the years, Poe backed away from his claim but remained bitter about the attention the hoax received and continued to poke holes in

Locke's shabby science if only to illustrate how unaccomplished it was even as a piece of fiction. The telescope, Poe calculated, was nowhere near powerful enough for Herschel to see what had been claimed. Still, Poe, who could be gracious only when he really tried, did admire what Locke had made:

> Not one person in ten discredited it, and (strangest point of all!) the doubters were chiefly those who doubted without being able to say why—the ignorant, those uninformed in astronomy, people who would not believe because the thing was so novel, so entirely "out of the usual way." A grave professor of mathematics in a Virginian college told me seriously that he had no doubt of the truth of the whole affair!

John Herschel, the real-life astronomer who unknowingly lent his good name and considerable fame to Locke's fiction, did not learn of the articles and his supposed discoveries until weeks later. News then traveled slowly, and Herschel was working in South Africa. By then, the hoax had been printed and reprinted, appearing in its pamphlet form in Hamburg, Naples, London, and Paris. Herschel expressed amusement and gratitude toward a few friends who came to his aid, declaring the articles fake. In an unsent letter to a London newspaper, written in 1836 but not discovered until 2001 and then published in the *Journal for the History of Astronomy*, Herschel said he believed "any person possessing the first elements of optical Science (to say nothing of Common Sense)" would not be misled by "the incoherent ravings . . . attributed to [him]." He feared though that even a ridiculous story, repeated widely, could come to be accepted as true. According to Samuel Johnson, Herschel continued, "There was nothing, however absurd or impossible which if seriously told a man every morning at breakfast for 365 days he would not end in believing—and it was a maxim of Napoleon that the most effective figure in Rhetoric is Repetition." Herschel's wife, Margaret, had more to say, writing her account of the events in a letter to her husband's aunt—also an astronomer (the whole family was forever looking up):

> Have you seen a very clever piece of imagination in an American Newspaper, giving an account of Herschel's voyage to the Cape with an Instrument [omitted] feet in length, & of his wonderful lunar discoveries? Birds, beasts & fishes of strange shape, landscapes of every colouring, extraordinary scenes of lunar vegetation, & groupes of the reasonable inhabitants of the Moon with wings at their backs, all pass in review before his & his companions' astonished gaze—The whole description is so well clenched with minute details & names of individuals boldly referred to, that the New Yorkists were not to be blamed for actually believing it. . . . It is only a great pity that it is not true, but if grandsons stride on as grandfathers *have* done, as wonderful things may yet be accomplished.

Optimism such as Margaret expresses in her letter was a necessary ingredient for the success of Locke's hoax. It was fuel for the brushfire. Hopes quiet doubts and, in doing so, make the extraordinary and fictional seem tenable, at hand, even, for a time, believable. Those "New Yorkists," many of them, believed what Locke wrote. This is another way of saying that they exhibited the general capacity or, perhaps better, the desire, to believe. They were optimistic people. They trusted that science made such discoveries possible. They hoped that such wild fancies might one day be matched by reality. And they had faith that progress, guided by the breakthroughs of astronomers, scientists, and doctors, awaited them in the future. They were, all told, easy marks. And yet, as Mrs. Herschel's letter makes clear, that same optimism underwrites exploration and scientific inquiry. It captures the hope that lands still lie undiscovered, unknown inventions may still be conceived, and unfound cures remain possible.

Yes, their hope that life existed on another planet—or, even nearer, on the moon—was misplaced and misinformed. Worse, it may have excused—or made it all too simple to ignore—the squalid conditions in the country's young cities and the looming political crisis over slavery, among many other wrongs in dire need of fixing. Their optimism was unfounded, but it offered the slim possibility of later escape when great problems in the United States and, more broadly, on Earth, overwhelmed the few simple solutions available. That hope may, for the crass and callow, have indicated the easy way out of a messy reality, allowing idle dreamers to slip into the realm of imagination, where consequences are unknown. That hope need not be so escapist or fanciful or even foolish. Rather, it might be understood instead as a critical impulse—call it a utopian urge— seldom remarked upon and less often respected, to try to form in the future a society that more closely matches Locke's bucolic vision, where to this day the buffalo still roam; to make lives better; and to improve, finally, on what is here and what is known for real.

A Good Story Is Hard to Find

An Interview with Michael Finkel

Michael Finkel had a great job. As a writer for the *New York Times Magazine*, he traveled widely, reporting on Haitian refugees, Palestinian youths, the brisk black market in human organs, and the cocoa trade in West Africa. In less than two years, he wrote eight features for the magazine, including two lengthy dispatches from the war in Afghanistan. He also contributed to the *Atlantic Monthly*, *National Geographic Adventure*, *Sports Illustrated*, and *Rolling Stone*.

Then, in February 2002, Finkel was fired. His editors at the *New York Times Magazine* published a note explaining that Finkel had, they discovered, created a composite character and used "improper narrative techniques" in his article about West Africa, "Is Youssouf Malé a Slave?" While reporting in Mali and the Ivory Coast, Finkel had interviewed many boys who worked in the cocoa fields, earned little money, and endured brutal working conditions, if not outright abuse. When writing and revising his article, however, Finkel blended details from the life of Malé, a real boy, with the experiences of others in similar straits.

The article that resulted from Finkel's experiment with truth and style was anything but standard magazine fare. Its spare language and hypnotic repetition owed as much to the plainspoken simplicity of folktales as the grit-flecked novels of Cormac McCarthy:

> The man came to the village on a moped. Youssouf Malé watched him. A man on a moped was unusual. When visitors did come to Nimbougou, deep in the hill country of southern Mali, they were almost always on foot, or on bicycle. The man on the moped had come to sell fabrics, the flower-patterned kind from which the women in Youssouf's village liked to sew dresses. Youssouf sat beneath a palm tree and watched.

Finkel did not so much tell Malé's story as channel the boy himself:

> And on this man's feet—my goodness. On this man's feet was something that Youssouf had never before seen. In Nimbougou, people either wore flip-flops or plastic sandals or nothing. What this man wore on his feet looked to Youssouf like a type of house. Like a miniature house, one for each foot. Two perfect, miniature houses, painted white, with curved walls that rose to the man's ankles, with a fence up the front of each one made of thin rope.

What followed the fake was the predictable storm: mea culpas and media criticism. Writers scolded the *New York Times* for allowing it to happen and roundly denounced Finkel, seeking in his personal life easy explanations for behavior they could not, it seemed, otherwise imagine. Some speculated, not very helpfully, that Finkel was under a great deal of stress. In Finkel's few statements to the media, he acknowledged his mistake but sought to keep it in the context of his entire career. "It's an isolated incident, without question a wrong decision," he told one reporter. "I hope readers know that this was an attempt to reach higher—to make something beautiful, frankly." Unlike Stephen Glass, a writer with whom he was sometimes compared, Finkel faked but once. When the *New York Times* subsequently re-reported all of Finkel's stories, the editors could find just two factual errors: the number of letters exchanged between two men was seven, not twenty, and a city's name was misspelled. Finkel retreated to his home in Montana and stopped writing for publications. To try to explain his silence, he told another reporter, "I have been doing a great deal of thinking, and I've decided to take some time before commenting further about the situation. Eventually, I plan to write about the experience myself."

In 2005, Finkel published *True Story,* a book that describes what he did, why, and also what happened next. Shortly after Finkel was fired, he learned that Christian Longo, a man suspected of murdering his wife and children, had taken Finkel's name and identity while on the run in Mexico. The coincidence was bizarre but true. The real and fake Finkels began exchanging lengthy personal letters after Longo was arrested and eventually met. Like Janet Malcolm's journalist and murderer, Finkel and Longo wanted something from each other. Finkel needed a story, a new assignment by which to prove himself and, perhaps, recuperate some of his lost credibility. Longo needed someone to talk to. Prison was lonely, after all, and Longo liked to talk, especially about himself. Finkel, a professional listener and a skeptic by nature, could, Longo realized, serve as a test audience, helping him to hone his alibis and explanations.

I interviewed Finkel by telephone on May 5, 2005 and, later that month, followed up with a few additional questions over e-mail.

Q. Why did you write about getting fired from the *New York Times Magazine* through the story of Christian Longo?

A. I figured that since I was fired, if I was ever going to write again, there was no way to write an article without saying somewhere in the first paragraph, "I really messed up. I know you know that I messed up, and I would like you to give me a second chance." Somehow address it, and I thought, here's a perfect way to do it.

Q. Shortly after losing your job, you told a reporter, "Eventually, I plan to write about the experience myself." What was it that you were planning to write then?

A. At that point, Chris Longo was nothing more than a fantastically coincidental diversion from my devastation and my deep depression, frankly, and self-loathing for what I had done. I had lost my job but not my reportorial instincts, so I immediately was curious about who would impersonate me. When I gave that quote to the reporter, I had no conception that what happened to me would be anything more than a journal entry. I thought I would just write about it in my journal to myself. In fact, what I was thinking, I believe, was you can take away my job and you can cut off my arms but I'll still find a way to write.

Q. For *True Story,* you explain that you fact-checked everything Longo told you, yet initially you could identify nothing amiss with his account. What does that suggest about the ability to catch people who are playing fast with the truth?

A. One of the themes of this book is this whole issue of what's true and what's not. What stories are true? What does "nonfiction" mean? What is thought of as good journalism? Accurate quotes? If I say to you, "I'm a girl named Jennifer," and then you report, "Mike Finkel is a girl named Jennifer," is that good journalism? It's an accurate quote, but it's completely false. You've not broken any rules of journalism, you've just written something completely false. That complexity is at the heart of this whole story.

Q. What's a reporter to do, then, when fact-checking fails?

A. I think what a reporter does is be honest with his or her readers and tell them this is an untrustworthy person. This is what I've been able to check. This is what I haven't. In the end, really, you can warn the reader and tell the story and let your readers decide how much is true and how much is false. There's not a lot you can do. You can't guarantee that everything in the story is true. You can only guarantee that it's accurate.

Q. Has Longo read the book?

A. I want him to read the book. I sent it to the Oregon State Penitentiary, where it was rejected. I sent it to his defense attorney in the hopes that it could be legitimately thought of as germane to his case. We have had a little contact lately, and I read him what I thought are the harshest indictments. He wasn't thrilled, but he wasn't unhappy. I think what he said to me was "That all sounds fair." Which is probably the best a journalist can hope for.

Q. While working on the West Africa story for the *New York Times Magazine*, you realized that many but not all of the reporters who covered it before you got it wrong. They wrote journalistically accurate stories, but they didn't capture the truth. An article in the *Chicago Sun-Times* said, "It was rare to meet a child who had not been beaten." Yet your experience was the exact opposite: beatings were rare.

A. The reporter didn't make that quote out of whole cloth. It was a quote given to him by an authority figure representing the laborers. I don't blame the reporter for using it. I may have used it myself. It's a powerful quote. Nobody has ever thought that journalists are infallible people. It just so happened that the very story that got me fired was a perfect example of accurate reporting in an untrue story. I think my West Africa story was completely accurate and untrue. I don't think reporters should be punished for being accurate and missing the story. It's just a demonstration that no matter how scrupulous you are, you can get fooled. Of course if somebody wants to fool you, they can fool you. But no reporter had any malicious intent.

Q. Why do you think people were outraged by your composite but couldn't have cared less about the reporters who got it wrong?

A. What I did was deliberate. I deliberately abused the readers' trust. People were upset with my mistakes and not others' because mine were done purposefully and theirs were absolutely innocent and completely understandable. That makes all the difference in the world.

Q. While you were working on the West Africa story, your editor suggested you "go literary." What did that instruction mean to you?

A. I want to emphasize right here that no editor at the *Times* told me to do anything improper and no editor was aware that I was doing anything improper. I knew exactly what she meant. She meant to write a magazine-style feature, to use the elements of literature that are acceptable in nonfiction—readability, flowery writing when necessary, metaphors, things like that. There was no implication to cheat.

Q. Your editor also suggested that you tell the story through one character, a boy. Why was that a good way to tell the story?

A. If I had a really great interview with one person who was representative of many, he would solve the problem of complexity right off the bat. You would have one character, which is very simple for a reader to keep in his or her mind, and then you can bring out a lot of the complexities. Nobody's going to make the mistake that every single boy is exactly the same. But there are enough similarities that by writing a detailed portrait of one boy, you can take an extraordinarily complex problem—the issues of abuse of children and child labor and West-East relations—and boil all that stuff away and let the reader focus on the telling details that illuminate the larger issues in a compelling, easily digestible way. It was a great idea to tell the story through one boy, and all I had to say was, "I don't have that story," and my editor immediately would have been fine with that. I have not ever forgiven myself for not just saying, "I don't really have that material." Because it really is a great idea. I wish that I had. I've berated myself about it repeatedly. Like I said, I've never fully forgiven myself. I wish I would have flown back to Africa and done it. I wish many things. I rue many things.

Q. That was an option, financially, to just say, "I don't have that story, but let me try again?"

A. I had written four pieces for the *Times* magazine in the previous year or so, and they were very well received, but in my ambition and paranoia, I'd forgotten all that. I was blindly ambitious and panicked that if I made one false move, I would be replaced. It's not like there's no one else who wants to write for the magazine. I realize now that all I had to do was be honest and open with my editor and there would be complete understanding. I might have written a mediocre story that they would have run. They might have killed it. But I think I would have continued to write for the magazine. Obviously, I didn't see that at the time.

Q. What other ways of telling the West Africa story did you try?

A. The article went through a few drafts, but right from the get-go, I was being deceptive and there was some compositing going on with the boy. I realized that I didn't have this great interview with a kid. So I decided, well, I'll write a profile of many people. I had a great interview with a plantation owner, and so I put him in. I had a great interview with a locateur, a person who transports the boys from one place to another. So I decided to put all those elements in place and show how no one person's to blame. It's like that Bob Dylan song, "Who Killed Davey Moore?" about a boxer who died in the ring. The locateur's just trying to make a dollar. The plantation owner's trying to do this. The boy's trying to earn a dime. I like to convince myself that if that draft was working, I would have cleaned it up. I was very frustrated. I had struggled with the writing. I was basically throwing things down. You know, it was such a rough draft. I was just trying to get the skeleton done.

Q. Both you and your editor wanted "a story that would sing." What does that mean?

A. It's an ineffable style and internal sense of propulsion that makes you want to go from one sentence to the next. It's like the difference between someone who can hit every key on the piano in the right order for the right amount of time, and someone who can *play* the piano. I wanted to combine nice prose and scrupulous accuracy with all my nonfiction pieces, without cheating.

Q. Are the literary qualities that people praise in nonfiction—these expectations for stories that sing, for dramatic lead paragraphs, interesting characters, and a central figure who, like a protagonist in a novel, can carry the whole narrative—difficult to balance with journalism's strict standards of truth?

A. Yes, they are. Let me give you one small example. If you look at all my articles together, there are never long passages of conversation. But sometimes I'm reading, like, "I'm driving my truck . . ." and there's this great conversation going on, and it's clearly not recorded and clearly the dude couldn't write it down, because he's driving his truck. I'm always either amazed they were able to remember it or skeptical that it was mostly re-created. I wonder how the writer can be so confident, to the point of using quotation marks, that that's how the conversation really went.

Q. What other elements of a good, engaging story are hard to capture while still writing an article that's journalistically sound?

A. Well, unless you're talking about birth and death, one's story does not have a smooth beginning and end. So, by nature, the beginning and the end are semi-artificial. What's really hard for me, writing in a magazine format, is to find a tale that feels complete and whole and yet is only two thousand words long. That, to me, is the hardest thing, a nice little chunk that fits into that space and doesn't leave too much out or oversimplify, that stays true and accurate and doesn't confound the reader. That's hard. But doable. I've written almost two hundred magazine articles. I'm able to do it.

Q. While working on *True Story*, how did you balance the obligations of telling a true story—being factually accurate—against telling a good story—being engaging and creating something that's a pleasure to read?

A. I was obsessed with those obligations, because of what happened to me, and because of the subject matter, and just because of the title of the book. It's very challenging almost. It's like: find a mistake in here. It took me three years of work to write this book. That's not fast. In fact, it's ridiculously slow. It's almost impossible for me to overstate how much I've thought about that conundrum, about writing a smooth, completely readable piece of writing and yet being absolutely beholden to the strictest rules of nonfiction.

There are aspects of nonfiction and fiction that are the same. Like you can write a nice metaphor in either one. Nice metaphors are not against the rules of nonfiction. Clean, readable sentences are not against the rules of nonfiction. Leaving out things, simplifying, is okay. Adding things is not. If I was writing fiction, this book would be smoother. If I was writing fiction, the characters would be more believable. If I was writing fiction, there would be a cleaner ending. But I'm not. So you have to learn that you're beholden to reality. That's your burden. Your benefit is that you don't have to invent an entire world. So it's both easier and harder. And you can have style and be a nonfiction writer. You just have to be careful. I was extremely careful during the three-year process of writing this book.

Q. The book is not as stylized as some of your journalism.

A. The book's style—or lack of style—was a natural choice. The material I'm working with sort of dictates which form of nonfiction storytelling to employ. In a lot of my journalism, there are devices. The device in my book is that there is no device. I completely bent over backwards to make sure that there was nothing like that.

Q. What are some of the devices you used before?

A. I've written with a "voice." The biggest example was in the story that got me fired, when I wrote in the voice of a young African laborer. I've also fiddled with structure—that is, not telling the story in a chronological way, but rather in a thematic order. The prime example was a piece I wrote about crossing the Sahara, "Thirteen Ways of Looking at a Void." It featured thirteen different people—tourists, natives, soldiers, drivers, etc.—telling their impressions of the vast ocean of sand at the center of the desert.

Q. Do you see yourself using devices again, or has the Youssouf Malé article made you suspicious of them?

A. It's made me more cautious and more self-conscious and possibly also a slower writer, but at the same time, I'm hoping that I can regain at least a majority of the readers' trust, and they'll know that anything like what happened with the *New York Times* will never happen again, and that if there's some sort of creative nonfiction used, it's only used in the most cautious and accurate way.

Q. Longo tells good stories, to you and others. They're believable on their face. But he can't really bring himself to tell his true story. What's the difference between good stories and true stories?

A. I feel like I won the lottery with the Longo story because the whole thing supports the exact themes I wanted to explore. As the West Africa case is perfect for explaining how you can be accurate and yet still get everything wrong, Longo himself is a perfect case for how someone can take all the checkable facts and make a completely false story out of it. Just about everything he said to me in fifty hours plus of phone interviews was either uncheckable or true. How perfect on one level and how profoundly annoying on another level.

When I was writing this book, one of the things I wanted to do was expose the inner workings of my reporting process. My magazine pieces sometimes are perhaps too slick, too smooth, and don't show how I reported them. In this book, I wanted not only to write the story, but say how I wrote the story, as if this was a watch with a clear face. You know, I'm telling the time, and here's how. I think there are enough flags to the readers. Hey, this part I checked. This part I couldn't. It's up to you to decide. This part felt genuine, but that's just a judgment call. This part felt like utter bullshit, as I said about his story on the stand. I mean, let's be honest, his story on the stand is absolutely factually accurate, but twelve jurors and I immediately didn't believe it. Is it possible that it's true? I guess it's possible the sun won't rise tomorrow. Did I believe it? Not at all. The whole question of what's true and what's not is exactly what the book is about. And I think by exposing the guts—by exposing the inner workings of my process—I think I'm giving the reader the ability to accept or reject Longo's story. I don't think I'm presenting it as the word of God.

Q. Is it hard to tell a true story that's also good?

A. It depends upon the subject. This book was difficult because of the subject and because of my past. I'm hoping that future stories will not be so difficult. I've been made more aware, more cautious, more suspicious, and yet a better reporter in the end.

The Specter of Hoaxes Past

When the November 1916 issue of the *New Republic* hit newsstands, it heralded the birth of an entirely new tradition of poetry: the "spectric school." This bold, unequivocal, even triumphant announcement stood out in the magazine's first books issue, a collection of reviews and essays solemn in tone and grudging with praise, interspersed with large dollops of bet-hedging. In the lead essay ("A Note on Criticism"), the editors jousted with imponderables such as "What rules have we for literature today?" They wondered, at length, whether standards were needed to improve criticism, or vice versa. They dilated on "temperament," "experience," and "the cultivated imagination." In one moment of uncharacteristic practicality, they warned against "the prevalence of bad taste, the success of charlatans, the vogue for jimcrackery."

Just a few pages later came extraordinary news of modern poetry's brightest hope, with none of the critical throat-clearing: "There is a new school of poets," the review began, "a new term to reckon with, a new theory to comprehend, a new manner to notice, a new humor to enjoy." The review, written by the poet Witter Bynner, put the nonsensical, exclamation point–riddled experiments of Emanuel Morgan and Anne Knish, the "cornerstone" and "keystone" of "spectra," into the context of go-go literary modernism and the artistic avant-garde of the day. Morgan, it seems, was an American expatriate and longtime painter who perfected his creative chops in Paris; Knish was born in Hungary, educated in Germany, and had lived all over Europe. Both had settled in Pittsburgh, where they prolifically turned out hundreds of spectric poems, all titled like classical music compositions (*Opus 76, Opus 29*, and so forth). They collected their best work in *Spectra*, a volume published that year.

Charged with reviewing their work, Bynner compared spectra to the other schools, all the other freshly minted –*isms*: namely, imagism, vorticism, and chorism (a misguided mixture of chant poetry and slow dancing championed by Ezra Pound). He found each wanting next to the newest state of the art. Imagist poems, Bynner argued, "give the . . . localized nervous sensations of a sick-bed, as though all the faculties were paralyzed except a finger-tip or one eye or one ear." A spectric poem, on the other hand, "goes deeper" and "cuts under mere technique."

What readers of that issue of the *New Republic* didn't know—what, for that matter, editors of the magazine, namely Herbert Croly and Philip Littell, didn't know—was that spectra wasn't so much a new mode of poetry as a hoax satirizing all the new modes. Nor was Bynner the "disinterested and impartial" reviewer called for in the issue's saber-rattling lead essay. Bynner was, in fact, Emanuel Morgan.

Spectra, a collection of inspired doggerel cum artistic manifesto for the nascent poetic movement, grew out of the shared complaints of Bynner and his friend Arthur Davison Ficke. Both had several serious bones to pick with the new poetry, in particular the sense that literary experimentation was rampant and unchecked and presently trampling all over poetry as they knew and loved it. Looking upon so much barbaric free verse loose across the land, they felt it incumbent on them to guard the gates. So, in Bynner's words, the two decided to have "fun with the extremists and with those of the critics who were overanxious to be in the van." Fueled by an antipathy for imagism and prodigious reserves of scotch, Bynner (writing as Morgan) and Ficke (as Knish) sequestered themselves in Davenport, Iowa, and Moline, Illinois, and in less than two weeks completed their manuscript. Still writing under their spectric pseudonyms, the poets sent a copy to the publisher Mitchell Kennerley, who had brought out books by both Bynner and Ficke. Kennerley accepted the manuscript and didn't flinch when the two briefly lifted their masks and revealed their true identities.

The hoax could easily have ended there, with the poets celebrating the publication of their book and the founding of their bogus school of expression. The potential audience for their hoax would have remained small, but the association with Kennerley at least would have guaranteed that the parodic poems found their way into small literary magazines. Yet through a chain of coincidences too tangled to explain here, Croly and Littell happened one day to see the page proofs for *Spectra* on Bynner's desk. Instead of recognizing the book as a fake, as Bynner thought they surely would, the editors saw what they wanted to see: evidence of a new, vigorous poetry. So much the better that nothing had yet been published about this brand new thing: the *New Republic* would be the first magazine on the bandwagon. Bynner, the editors decided, had to review *Spectra* for them.

The details of Bynner's and Ficke's deft, large-scale forgery, as well as the original collection of the poems by Morgan and Knish, are presented in William Jay Smith's highly engaging *The Spectra Hoax*, first published in 1961 and brought back into print, with an updated preface, in 2000. Smith is a careful literary detective with a clear sense of what's funny and absurd about the spectric duo. He fingers the poets' feisty targets, the duped writers, and those who slipped through the net. He also describes the hoax's eventual unmasking more than two years later. But in Smith's account, the hoax is decidedly and solely literary; its effects are limited and do not reverberate outside the literary world. Bynner and Ficke simply concocted a new, highly preposterous and pretentious school to mock what they saw as preposterous, pretentious, and ultimately bankrupt in all the other schools. They lampooned modernism's excesses. The era's unbridled artistic experimentation and criticism's lagging vocabulary and grasp of the new art gave the spectric authors all the license they needed. Yes, their critique was sharp and their irony cutting, but they only cut fellow poets, editors of literary magazines, critics, and reviewers.

The question of how so much spectric jimcrackery infiltrated a magazine as influential as the *New Republic* does not interest Smith. In *The Spectra Hoax*, the magazine's editors are hoodwinked because the era had already primed them to expect and accept strange artistic phenomena. Smith makes nothing of a painfully glaring irony—that the spectra hoax appeared cheek by jowl with a call to critical arms. Nor, although he quotes from nearly all the spectric poets' contemporary reviews, favorable or not, does Smith pay much attention to the stampede of magazines, newspapers, and journals to fall into line behind Croly and Littell. Nothing is more remarkable about the hoax than the efficiency and ease with which the *New Republic* made the new poetry, this fake phenomenon, tip, as Malcolm Gladwell would have it. A Republican nominee for mayor of Newark, for example, in what must be one of the strangest recorded evasions of political issues, read aloud from *Spectra* at campaign appearances.

It's too bad Smith doesn't reach for deeper interpretations, because much more is at stake in the spectra hoax than two poets' aggrieved sense that free verse got out of control way back when. So while Smith is busy pointing at the Beat poets and, in the new edition, John Ashbery, as evidence that we need spectra-like satire more than ever to stop the creep of artistic decadence and formlessness, a more interesting and more relevant tale goes untold: the story of the sometimes deliberate and sometimes unwitting collaboration of the news media in perpetuating hoaxes. Journalists' unending infatuation with being the first to report on the latest fad, newest craze, or most *avant* of avant-garde cultural expressions makes them easy prey to hoaxes that give even a hint of promising entrée to, say, a formerly underexplored strain of youth culture, music, or cutting-edge business or technology.

The specter of hoaxes past hangs over journalists today, particularly those on quests for the next new thing. Bynner and Ficke's shenanigans help explain why, in 1997, a reporter for *Nightline*, who was working on a segment about the then-newfangled Internet, believed the cyber-inflected hamming of Joshua Glenn, editorial director of the Web site Tripod. "Ramp it up," Glenn exhorted in ersatz digitalese. "Get the synergies ramping with daily rocket." He was speaking, for all the reporter and her producers knew, in an exotic, rarely recorded language, and she was lucky enough to capture this coded expression for a television audience forever fascinated, supposedly, by whatever passes for rare glimpses at anything. Along similar lines, the editors of *Social Text* did not doubt physicist Alan Sokol's intentions in writing about the culturally constructed nature of, say, gravity. If anything they felt subtly congratulated to learn a scientist shared so many of their hoary postmodern commonplaces.

The *New Republic* of Croly and Littell is, finally, not so far removed from the *New Republic* of Charles Lane and Michael Kelly, who eagerly embraced rogue staff writer Stephen Glass and his visions of reality. Glass's now-infamous article about the bratty fifteen-year-old hacker demanding money, a convertible, a rare comic book, and a lifetime supply of pornography offered, for lifelong journalists and shut-in editors, glimpses into the workings of a high-tech computer firm, a land as foreign and bewildering to Lane and Kelly as the new poetry was to Croly and Littell. Glass's editors had heard rumors, of course, about how computer programmers could name their price, and the conventional wisdom, after all, maintained that the young do possess special powers over computers and electronic devices. In the end, what's poetic about the spectra hoax is how elegantly it demonstrates that any new writing, from reporting to reviewing to intellectual journalism, finds the easiest path to publication by seeking the consensus and falling into the deep groove of what's already written and held to be true.

Poetic Invention

Monsters get confused with their makers. Frankenstein, the daring doctor with the bold ideas, devised an experiment and made a monster for himself, but while the character Mary Shelley described as a modern Prometheus gave life to this "wretch" stitched together from body parts scavenged from fresh graves, he did not bother to give the thing a name. He certainly never granted the monster use of his good name. Still, the monster, surprisingly human, its behavior like a real man's, its movements so lifelike, needed an identity. The popular imagination filled this blank with a simple mistake: Frankenstein is the monster, and the scientist merely mad. The monster has eclipsed the maker.

Peter Carey's novel *My Life as a Fake*, which begins with an epigraph from Shelley's book and, like any globe-spanning adventure tale, defies easy summary, tells the story of an author—a kind of literary Frankenstein really—who looses on the world a monster. In 1946, Christopher Chubb, an Australian poet, creates a fake poet named Bob McCorkle and manages to get his work published in a journal. The editor is deeply embarrassed, just as Chubb intended, and the journal discredited. The editor dies under mysterious circumstances and suspicion falls, naturally, on Chubb. A stranger appears, as only strangers in Dickens and Carey can, disrupting everyone's life and sowing havoc. This stranger is "a massive man with wild dark eyes and black, shoulder-length hair." He claims to be McCorkle, the nonexistent poet, and, furthermore, insists that he is the author of the fake poetry. McCorkle has business with Chubb. He demands from his maker a birth certificate, an identity, and proof of his existence, the better to be free and his own man. Then he kidnaps from Chubb his only daughter and convinces her that her father is the impostor.

Twenty-six years later, in 1972, Sarah Wode-Douglass, the novel's narrator and editor of a high-toned poetry magazine supported by W.H. Auden and other swells, and John Slater, a poet famous for his writing when young but now mostly infamous for his long history of romantic affairs, travel to Kuala Lumpur and unexpectedly encounter Chubb. He's a shell of a man, with untreated sores on his legs and the furtive, nervous manner of an animal accustomed to hiding. Chubb has one suit of clothes, which heavy rains destroy. He works in the back of a small store repairing bicycles and, when time permits and his hands aren't too greasy, reading a little Rilke. Chubb tells his story to Wode-Douglass and Slater, Ancient Mariner–style, which is to say at great, uninterrupted length. The editor is entranced and quickly becomes obsessed. Chubb shows her a poem by McCorkle, just for a few seconds, and she wants to read more, desperately; though she knows McCorkle to be a fake and Chubb less than trustworthy, she believes the poem she read to be a masterpiece.

My Life as a Fake is not Carey's best novel. Moments of sharply drawn metaphor—he describes Chubb's mouth, for example, as "tight and small as a widow's purse"; elsewhere, music from a nearby disco sounds "like some creature thumping its great flat tail against the earth"—are many, but the novel suffers from a fundamental structural flaw: Chubb's story fascinates; Chubb's telling of his story in the novel's present does not. Wode-Douglass and Slater have little to occupy them in the novel save to listen and, in the editor's case, take notes; until, that is, the very end, when they're drawn into a plot so filled with last-minute incident and rushed explanation that it reads like the conclusion to a bad movie—part horror, part James Bond.

Carey's novel is something of a fake itself, artfully based on and, at times, directly lifted from a real literary hoax that unfolded in Australia in 1944, when James McAuley and Harold Stewart, two published poets, got fed up with what they viewed as the excesses of modernism and so invented a poet named Ern Malley, whose writing embraced every literary value they could not stand. Carey's previous novel, the Booker Prize–winning *True History of the Kelly Gang*, was based on real events as well, bringing to life the Australian outlaw Ned Kelly. Historical novels relate plausible but ultimately fake histories, and their authors labor tirelessly to fashion simulations of the past that can pass for real, doling out just enough fact to convince readers to believe their fiction. Carey, however, simulates the historical past with more than the accurate terminology for the furniture and the architecture and a few knowing references to gaslight lamps. He creates fake versions of the past by attending to his characters' language, manners, interior lives, and—an eighteenth-century word—sensibilities. Details are the faker's closest friend and the basis for any persuasion, and so Carey fills in the crevices of his eight novels and one book of stories with an embarrassment of rich particulars, imagining cultures in their entirety: their vocations, churches, politics, police, and, absent from most contemporary novels, social classes. Carey's fictional characters never reside in sparse worlds.

The real poetry hoax, which Carey has said he remembers hearing about while growing up, lacked the gothic elements— the monster, the beautiful daughter of indeterminate parentage, the guilt thickening the air. It also lacked the well-oiled machinery of dramatic payback that Carey constructs, it sometimes seems, to sex up a plot and characters that might otherwise come off as bookish or dry. After all, literary hoaxes and literary concerns are not generally matters of life and death, however much writers and editors can carry on as if they were. And justice makes a mess of the world as much as it restores order or rights wrongs. It can be slow and uncertain, even timid and incorrect. All of which is to say that poets pursuing their art, however ambitious, do not often rack up a body count. Furthermore, justice rarely if ever appears so poetic and harsh as a hoaxer meeting his invention face-to-face and then being tormented and stalked by him for years and across several countries, only to be left for ruin, a broken man.

The Ern Malley Affair is Michael Heyward's wonderful and exhaustive account of the hoax that inspired Carey, the fake poet, and the actual aftermath. It stars men instead of monsters and concludes with stunted, uncertain literary careers in lieu of death. Heyward's book was never published in the United States and has gone regrettably out of print since it was first published in England in 1993. He weighs the hoaxers' satiric intentions against the earnest interpretations of the hoaxed, never failing to be fair and judicious. Carey, however, rules on the case of the hoaxer like a hanging judge, rigidly moral and unsparing with his punishment. When the narrator of *My Life as a Fake* learns of the hoax for the first time, she immediately reflects that the hoaxer "preyed on the best, most vulnerable quality an editor has to offer . . . that hopeful, optimistic part which has you reading garbage for half your life just so you might find, one day before you die, a great and unknown talent." Much later, once the narrator has had a chance to get to know the hoaxer personally, she compares him to "a soul in hell, like a prisoner turning the capstan in the drowning room, forever indentured to something to which he himself had given birth."

McAuley and Stewart, the real hoaxers, never endured circumstances so grim, though they did serve in the Australian Army. McAuley was a lieutenant and Stewart a corporal, and owing to their education and sheer luck, both held desk jobs during World War II at the Directorate of Research and Civil Affairs. It was a cushy assignment. They taught the infantry about the dangers of malaria in New Guinea, where mosquitoes felled more troops than Japanese soldiers. Such work, while important, was not always demanding, and so on an otherwise uneventful Sunday, McAuley and Stewart decided to invent their bad poet, write his bad poems—a whole manuscript, in fact, titled *The Darkening Ecliptic*—and present their creation to an unsuspecting literary world.

Their target was specific. Their satire was to be as precise as surgery. They mailed the manuscript to Max Harris, the high-flying and, some said, arrogant editor of *Angry Penguins*, a literary magazine dedicated to the principles of modernism and surrealism, the more obscure and dense and nonsensical the better. *Angry Penguins* was a plush, well-produced publication, and Harris was never shy about finessing a connection with James Laughlin, who helped him acquire new work from Dylan Thomas, Kenneth Rexroth, and other poets in the New Directions stable. To artists and writers in Europe Harris's pet *-isms* were already long in the tooth, but in Australia the ideas retained a newness and freshness sufficient to inspire artists to contest their merits and debate their values. In 1939, an exhibit of paintings by Picasso, Matisse, and Chagall toured the country; for many Australians, this was their first chance to see examples of European modern art outside reproductions in books. Where artists in Europe by then treated modernism and surrealism as two pieces of the establishment's furniture— there for them to sit on and rearrange however they liked— Australia's artists remained skeptical and, for the most part, conservative and traditional.

McAuley and Stewart, for instance, each wrote poetry in strict meter, and while they appreciated Picasso and some Eliot (not "The Waste Land"), they drew the line somewhere well shy of Dylan Thomas and his "force that through the green fuse drives the flower." They were not antimodernists so much as opposed to a certain kind of deliberately opaque, second-generation modernism whose practitioners worked under the banners of symbolism, neoromanticism, or new apocalypticism—poets who are now forgotten. Reviewing Harris's poetry in 1942,

Stewart described it as "semi-surrealist verse" and "first rough drafts," work that "any poet of talent could produce a hundred lines of . . . a week for the rest of his life." Such writing, according to Stewart, was "no harder to do than a free-association test."

In Adelaide, meanwhile, the most conservative city in southern Australia, Harris served proudly as the standard-bearer for the causes of cultural experimentation, avant-gardism, and left-wing politics. Those causes attracted a small but dedicated following in Australia. A new issue of *Angry Penguins* might be read by about nine hundred people, give or take. Not that a small circulation necessarily connoted irrelevance or a lack of influence: John Ashbery told Heyward he found copies stocked at the Grolier Poetry Bookshop, in Cambridge, while he was an undergraduate at Harvard.

Ern Malley's poems reached Harris's desk through the kindness of Ethel Malley, the fake poet's fake sister. Her brother had died, Ethel explained in her first letter, and while she didn't know a thing about poetry ("I am no judge of it myself. . . . I am not a literary person and I do not feel I understand what he wrote") and confessed that she hadn't even known that her brother wrote poems, a friend had prevailed on her to submit them anyway. Harris liked Malley's work—he was, he said, "very much impressed"—and responded with enthusiasm, writing to communicate his intention to publish it and asking Ethel to send any more writing by her brother that she could find. Ethel mailed Harris the rest of *The Darkening Ecliptic* along with an overly serious and almost funny "Preface and Statement" that is as unnecessary ("These poems are complete") as it is repetitive ("These poems are complete in themselves") and opaque ("There are no scoriae or unfulfilled intentions"). Ethel also included a long letter describing her brother's quiet, desperate life. Ern Malley's poems get all the attention, predictably, but Ethel's letters bear the brunt of the hoax's work, alone creating a well-rounded character in whom Harris would believe. The poems were a temptation for Harris, like beautiful fruit dangling from a tree, but Ethel's letters led him to the grove. Her writing is perfect—flat but not too, and never obviously bad—while her voice mixes equal parts love for her brother and a credible lack of interest in poetry.

Her brother, Ethel wrote, had dropped out of high school and lived alone in a rented room in south Melbourne, working variously as an auto mechanic, a life insurance salesman, and a watch repairer until his death at age twenty-five, from complications caused by Graves' disease. On the side, when he had time, Malley was Australia's most experimental and audacious poet, penning such lines as "A pallid polka or a yelping shimmy / Over these sunken sodden breeding-grounds!" in a poem inspired by McAuley's and Stewart's jobs at the directorate and the many books about mosquitoes they had on hand. Malley also committed to paper "Hawk at the wraith / Of remembered emotions" and "Knowst not, my Lucia, that he / Who has caparisoned a nun dies / With his twankydillo at the ready?" Carey, perhaps fearing the artistic vertigo that might result from trying to create fake nonsense that lives up to such older fake nonsense, wisely just gives several of Malley's poems whole to his poet. And so, in the manner of Don Quixote and his crafty Borgesian imitator Pierre Menard, both poets, McAuley's and Stewart's fake and Carey's fictional fake, write "Boult to Marina," which begins:

Only a part of me shall triumph in this
(I am not Pericles)
Though I have your silken eyes to kiss
And maiden-knees
Part of me remains, wench, Boult-upright
The rest of me drops off into the night.

The hoaxers' poems appeared, in their entirety, in the Autumn 1944 issue of *Angry Penguins*, an issue published "To Commemorate the Australian Poet Ern Malley." Artist Sidney Nolan, the magazine's designer, painted the cover after reading one of Malley's poems ("Dear we shall never be that verb / Perched on the sole Arabian tree"). After learning Malley didn't exist, Nolan painted a speculative portrait, imagining the poet in a wide-brimmed hat and wire-rimmed glasses, his eyes two different colors and his tongue hanging out like a panting dog's. Within days of the magazine's appearance, academics cried fake, or satire, or they weren't sure what, exactly. A professor of literature at Adelaide University who was sympathetic to modernist poetry suspected Harris of parodying himself as a way of repudiating his youthful dalliances with experimental literature, namely the novel called *The Vegetative Eye*, which wags referred to as *Vegetable Pie*. Another critic simply thought the work derivative of writing in past issues. Interested parties, and there were more than a few, set out to discover what they could about Malley. Harris hired a private investigator to stake out the house where Ethel supposedly lived, and reporters at Australian newspapers and magazines, sensing the presence of a lively story about something other than the interminable war, began to snoop.

McAuley and Stewart meanwhile didn't want to call it quits just yet. They were eager to unveil that their unschooled poet was also an unschooled artist. Ern Malley, their greatest creation, was dead, sure, taken early like John Keats, but they wanted the hoax to live on, at least a bit longer. Hoping to fool another unsuspecting surrealist, Stewart fashioned a dozen collages, not-entirely-sophisticated knockoffs of Ernst and Magritte, clipping the images from the pages of *National Geographic*, pasting them together, and giving the pieces pun-riddled or artsy names like *Malice in Underland* and *Rococo Interior*, which features a disproportionately large toilet installed in a palace ballroom. The hoaxers realized, though, that events were about to render obsolete their well-laid plans. Articles, they knew, would run in the newspapers regardless of their cooperation, and so they worried, for good reason, that if they remained silent, nobody would ever understand their motivations. The hoaxers dropped their scissors and glue, hastily revised their plans, and set about concocting an artistic statement to explain their intentions.

The reporters, in truth, didn't care much about the hoaxers' intentions. Modernism was, to them, a mystery best left unsolved. McAuley and Stewart revealed themselves, gave interviews, and gamely fielded phone calls from reporters. They had described their plans at length, chiefly in the form of an open letter and manifesto, but reporters found the writing impossible to publish in full and not easy to understand or summarize. The story, as it appeared in the Adelaide *Mail* and *Fact*, the magazine of the Sunday *Sun*, and elsewhere, dealt only casually with what the hoaxers viewed as modernism's excesses and how they believed surrealism went wrong. The satire was less important than the scandal. Distressed, McAuley and Stewart watched their aesthetic argument, the careful critique of avant-garde poetry, grow blunter with each new article.

Those articles told a story far easier to write and sell: poetry is a folly and all these poets are fools. Lost were the subtleties of motivation. Harris, for example, appeared as a simple dupe, not as a person who wanted to believe, as any editor does, that he had discovered in his slush pile a great unknown, an Australian Keats, unappreciated even by his own family. What's more, Harris needed to believe that his aesthetic impulses already had a champion among the working class. If Malley, a humble garage mechanic with little formal education, understood that the future of writing lay in surrealist experiments and a fearless exploration of the subconscious, then the battle was won, the war over, and the traditionalists vanquished along with their metered lines. Soon, as Harris dreamed, Australian poets might catch up to their heady European betters. To the public, however, Malley's work was less literary than simply ludicrous, and his sorry tale less an ingenious hoax than a naughty scandal and a welcome diversion from bloodshed. The only *–ism* the reporters appreciated, it seemed, was sensationalism. The hoax was out of hand.

Each week 250,000 people turned to *Fact*, and each week the editors delivered a steady diet of lurid tales, oddball feats of human achievement, and garden-variety exploitation. On the same page as the first of *Fact's* two-part exposé about Ern Malley, readers found a regular favorite, the latest dish about the murderer of a child the editors had dubbed "Pyjama Girl." The hoaxers, according to Heyward, had no idea what they had wrought:

Shocks, of a mild degradable kind, were *Fact*'s business. McAuley and Stewart had not anticipated how well Ern would make model copy for pap. In the event, publication in *Fact* maximized the titillation of the hoax and stymied debate. . . . The publication of McAuley's and Stewart's stern statement in *Fact* brought the goofy side of the hoax into sharp relief. Ern becomes a passing freak, a lifeless wonder. . . . And Ern fulfills a principle that poetry merits publicity when it generates gossip about its own strangeness—in this case at the moment when, supplanted by the story of its composition, it ceases to exist.

Within a couple of months, articles about the hoax appeared in the *New York Times*, *Time*, *Newsweek*, *The Nation*, and the *New Yorker*. For Harris, the hoax and the sheaf of bad publicity took a turn for the far worse when a vindictive prosecutor in Adelaide brought obscenity charges against him for the publication of the Malley poems. Harris now had to defend his literary judgment. He testified for days, refusing to speculate as to the intentions of a nonexistent poet but nonetheless being forced to explain, in court, how he personally went about interpreting these strange poems. One characteristic line of questioning concerned the phrase "Boult-upright." Did that or did that not in fact refer to an erection? The case was ridiculous, and the transcripts of the trial read like an absurdist play, but trumped-up charges are still charges. Harris, who found little to laugh at and much to worry over, got off with a small fine and a great deal of public humiliation.

The hoaxers had thought they were tossing a dart at a small magazine, a well-intentioned pinprick aimed to pop its fatuous bubble. Like the poets behind the spectra hoax, concocted to send up imagism and its acolytes, McAuley and Stewart were serious about their project. And like the writer behind Araki Yasusada, a fictional survivor of Hiroshima whose oeuvre, entirely fabricated, was nonetheless published, in the mid-1990s, in the *American Poetry Review*, *Grand Street*, and *Conjunctions*, McAuley and Stewart didn't like to see their work as Malley called a mere hoax or, worse, a prank, preferring the more earnest term "experiment." Their point, regardless of its name, was a narrow and strictly literary one, couched expressly for a specialized audience. Satire need not be so small in its effects, but it should always cut with subtlety and swiftness. As word of the hoax got out, however, reporters replayed the dart as a cannon and the pinprick as the opening salvo in a new, albeit less dangerous, cultural war between the avant-garde and traditionalists, thus rendering the hoaxers' narrow point impossibly broad and making both sides out to be laughingstocks and clowns. In *My Life as a Fake*, Carey's sympathies are largely with Harris and *Angry Penguins* and their fictional proxies, David Weiss and his magazine *Personae*, not because he necessarily identifies with their aesthetic program of surrealism for the masses but because he sees them as morally wronged. Weiss dies as a result of the hoax, and much of the remainder of the novel reads like a cruel and elaborate addition to Dante's hell: a new circle Carey devises expressly to take care of writers who make monstrous fakes.

Harris stuck by his belief that Ern Malley was a great poet, even if his creators remained bad poets themselves, hopelessly mired in their outdated, traditional ways. McAuley and Stewart, for their equally stubborn part, resisted the idea that Malley's poems had any value other than to make a satiric point about the emptiness of Harris's surrealist aesthetics. From the first day the hoax was revealed, Harris predicted that Malley's work would demonstrate that "the myth is sometimes greater than its creator." And by most standard measures of literary renown, Harris's words have become true: The myth has eclipsed the makers. Today Malley does outshine McAuley and Stewart; his work was included in a prominent U.S. anthology of Australian poetry shortly after its original publication, and it has since been reprinted many times. In 1961, *Locus Solus*, the avant-garde literary magazine edited by Ashbery, Harry Mathews, Kenneth Koch, and James Schuyler, republished two poems by Malley. Ashbery sometimes gave his students a copy of a Malley poem along with work by a real, earnest modernist, an experiment to test whether they could tell the work of a well-regarded contemporary writer from a spoof. Only about half identified the Malley correctly. As for Ashbery, he admired Malley's poems. "They reminded me a little of my own early tortured experiments in surrealism," he said, "but they were much better." Time and literary fashion look kindly on *The Darkening Ecliptic*. What must have read as outrageous in Australia in the 1940s will, for readers of Ashbery or any number of contemporary poets, seem rather tame now.

The hoax poems are still, in the end, poems. They look every bit like real poems. When read, they sound like poems, albeit nonsensical for long stretches. The hoaxers thought them bad, but someone else thought them good. The hoaxers believed their experiment revealed, once and for all, the utter bankruptcy of a magazine's aesthetics; the editor believed he discovered something rare. McAuley and Stewart said the poems were doggerel, and Harris asked others to appreciate their greatness. Is Harris a fool for believing so? Are the hoaxers mistaken about their own efforts? Is intention nothing? And is opinion all?

Awakened one night after midnight by a reporter hungry for an embarrassing quotation, Harris provided perhaps his most cogent defense. Asked what he would say if told that the makers of Malley claimed their intentions were wholly satirical, Harris replied, "The history of literature is paved with intentions producing contradictory results." Imagine that every artist who ever intended to paint a masterpiece managed somehow to do so. The museums would be many and their walls crowded. So if a writer can sit down with every intention, hope, and prayer of composing a masterpiece and instead make only a mess, surely the opposite can occur. The hoaxers, after all, did not mail Harris a crate of oranges and watch him, the fool, publish their freshly picked fruit as if they were sonnets. He merely read their poems and liked them, and, liking them, he chose to publish them. In an author's note at the end of *My Life as a Fake*, Carey quotes from a letter Harris wrote years after the hoax. "I still believe in Ern Malley," he wrote. "Most of you probably didn't think about the story of Ern Malley's life. It got lost in the explosive revelation of the hoax. . . . It was not likely you closed your eyes and tried to conjure up such a person as the mythical Ern Malley . . . a garage mechanic suffering from the onset of Graves' Disease." Harris continued, reassembling the character of Malley, rebuilding him, body and mind, out of his own words this time, constructing him not as a hoax but as a man, a poet who submitted his work to a magazine. "I can still close my eyes," Harris added, "and conjure up such a person in our streets."

Carey's sympathies, as capacious and all-embracing as any working novelist's, do extend eventually to Malley and the hoaxers. Malley is a character that has lasted, as Carey must recognize. Malley lives. He's alive. And like a monster, he's taken on a life of his own. Like a character, he's a welcome addition to literature, and if a couple of hoaxers made him, thanks be to them. McAuley and Stewart composed their poems in a rush, they say, from fragments of thoughts, bad ideas, and random phrases, mangled quotations, misattributed citations, and reports on mosquitoes. Whether or not the verse that results from their inventive methods can stand as a masterpiece, Ern Malley, their creation, the poet and mechanic living and working in isolation and then dying young, remains a wonderful character—a fake, in other words, or perhaps better to say, a careful imitation of a man whose life many readers may still wish to believe is real.

Hoaxes without End

An Interview with Joey Skaggs

On April 13, 1844, the *New York Sun* published a special edition, called the *Extra Sun*, on the strength of a front-page story announcing that a hot air balloon had successfully crossed the Atlantic Ocean. With no fewer than eight exclamation points and a series of bold headlines, subheads, and kickers that filled one-third of the column, the *Sun* trumpeted its astounding news. The balloon had crossed the Atlantic in three days! The "Flying Machine!!!" had just arrived and landed in Charleston, South Carolina. The article promised "full particulars of the voyage!!!" The article, as it happens, was fictional. It was written by Edgar Allan Poe and published knowingly by the *Sun*. New York newspapers were far more numerous then and competition for readers was fierce, so Poe's story was a surefire way for the *Sun*'s editors to boost the paper's circulation. They were right; the *Sun* sold fifty thousand copies of the special edition. Poe was amazed and, even stranger for him, genuinely overjoyed at the enthusiasm that greeted his story. He wrote:

> On the morning (Saturday) of its announcement, the whole square surrounding the 'Sun' building was literally besieged, blocked up—ingress and egress being alike impossible, for a period soon after sunrise until about two o'clock P.M. [. . .] I never witnessed more intense excitement to get possession of a newspaper. As soon as the first copies made their way into the streets, they were bought up, at almost any price, from the news-boys, who made a profitable speculation.

Today, Poe's fictional news article appears in most of the major collections of his writing, as a story called "The Balloon-Hoax." His story came to mind as I was preparing to interview Joey Skaggs, an artist who has, since 1976, made up stories that are the contemporary equivalent of Poe's and managed to get them published in newspapers and on the Internet and broadcast on television and the radio, all without editors and reporters suspecting a thing.

In 1999, Skaggs created the Final Curtain, a fake company, and its requisite Web site, which promised to build cemeteries on the model and scale of theme parks, complete with restaurants, gift shops, and something called the "timeshare greenhouse." The company got quite a bit of attention in the media before Skaggs revealed it as his latest hoax. Thinking about Skaggs and Poe, I wondered about the fifty thousand people who had bought that issue of the *Sun*. Were they just hoodwinked? Was it that simple? Or did they also come away with a story, albeit fictional, about progress, human achievement, and risky adventures, all of which they happened to want to believe? And could the same be said for those of us fooled by a Skaggs hoax today, or tomorrow?

I interviewed Skaggs by e-mail in July and August 2000.

Q. Now that you've revealed the Final Curtain, I'd like you to talk about some of the logistical nitty-gritty that goes into one of your productions.

A. The Final Curtain took about two years of work from when I first started putting it together to when I released the exposé. Having come up with the concept to satirize the funeral industry, I decided to create a bogus company and Web site to promote the concept. I wanted to use the Internet because while fact and fiction are so easily manipulated and blurred, it has also become an ubiquitous and supposedly reliable source for information. It gave us an instantaneous and constant presence, with the illusion of having a history. I registered a domain name and put together a team of volunteers. In this case, over fifty people helped perpetrate the hoax—businesspeople, writers, architects, Web designers, programmers, ISP providers, and the artists who provided concepts and sketches for their monuments.

We created the Final Curtain Web site complete with architectural renderings, a development proposal, biographies for the management team, information about investment opportunities and the timeshare program for the deceased, a monument gallery of iconoclastic and satirical grave sites and urns, and a tour of the memorial theme park.

To be successful, this project had to appear completely real. I needed a mailing address, letterhead, telephone business listing, and a staff. One volunteer agreed to let me use his home office address in New Jersey and we installed a telephone line under the name of Investors Real Estate Development d/b/a the Final Curtain.

All calls and mail were forwarded to my New York City studio. Our Webmaster created e-mail addresses for all the staff members which were also routed to me. They were real people, but since none had the time to deal with the day-to-day correspondence once the piece took off, I played all the roles.

Then I placed ads in twenty alternative newspapers around the country. The ad read, "Death got you down? At last an alternative! www.finalcurtain.com."

Q. What initial reactions did you get from the ads?

A. As soon as the ads came out, the hits to the site spiked into the tens of thousands per day for several weeks. However, only a few people responded directly.

Q. Then what happened?

A. I let the Final Curtain percolate. Over the next six months, we added artists' submissions to the Monument Gallery. This helped it look as if it had caught on and that more people were becoming involved.

When I felt the site was sufficiently populated with creative, emotionally poignant monuments, I launched a major PR campaign announcing the concept and soliciting artists' monuments for a scholarship program. The winners would receive free ten-foot by ten-foot plots for their memorials or urns at one of our soon-to-be-created memorial theme parks.

Q. Satire always seems to require at least some of the audience to completely miss what's funny and accept it as real. Were these very serious, earnest submissions from artists who took the Web site at face value?

A. The responses I got seemed genuinely sincere. Some artists embraced the concept and were happy to participate.

Others saw it as a business opportunity. For example, one artist who did tombstone engraving for people and pets wanted to put her work up in the gallery as a way to get more work through the Final Curtain.

Q. So next the Final Curtain starts to get early attention from the media.

A. The media response kept me extremely busy granting interviews. I played various staff members and appeared on radio shows, in newspapers and magazines, on the Internet, and on TV shows. Thankfully no one asked me to come in to the studio.

After an article appeared in the *Los Angeles Times*, the legal challenges began. A lawyer for Uncle Milton Industries, Inc., owner of the registered trademark "Ant Farm," sent a formal complaint to both the writer at the *Los Angeles Times* and our company claiming trademark infringement because one artist's monument emulated an ant farm.

It pays to have a pro bono lawyer friend with a sense of humor. In response we changed the language on the site to "ant habitat," and all was well with the world again. But I couldn't pass up the opportunity to stir up a little more trouble. I sent a second press release out about the ant farm controversy to keep the Final Curtain in the news.

Q. The fact that Uncle Milton's attorneys took the Final Curtain seriously became justification for journalists just hearing about the Final Curtain to take it seriously, too.

A. When something seemingly adverse happens, I use it as an opportunity. Controversies help to distract reporters from questioning the original premise.

Q. Then what happened?

A. Months went by and I maintained nine-to-five business

hours, pretending I worked in a real office. I handled a flood of interviews by phone and e-mail. I had an answering machine with a secretary's voice on the message, so I could occasionally leave "the office."

I tape-recorded and logged all the calls, and kept track of the articles and stories through print and electronic clipping services. I had to keep everything going long enough for numerous magazines, with very long lead times, to publish their stories.

Q. In order to create a fictional business you had to behave like an actual business. You kept business hours, you held meetings with your volunteers, you did all those standard business things. It's as if some semblance of reality can't be imitated accurately without re-creating reality completely. Running a business that's supposed to appear real could even be harder than running a real business.

A. When I create a false reality, I always try to create a plausible structure to help convince people.

Q. When and why did you decide to reveal the hoax?

A. After many months of running this nonexistent company, I was satisfied with the success of the piece. I composed and mailed an exposé press release. I canceled the auxiliary telephone line and mounted a disclaimer on the Final Curtain Web site. But releasing an exposé doesn't mean the piece is over. Since a majority of the media that had fallen for it chose not to do a follow-up and never revealed it was a hoax, many people weren't exposed to the truth. Consequently some serious inquiries continued to come in. Even with a disclaimer on the Web site, I receive letters of inquiry, commentary, and offers.

Q. As you watch the news or read newspapers, what do you notice about journalism that you then take into account in your hoaxes? Are there types of stories reporters tend to go for that you then try to replicate?

A. Sometimes it's a matter of being topical and outrageous. Other times you can use a calendar to predict the kinds of stories the media is looking for. Celebrations of anniversaries of disasters, such as nuclear power plant meltdowns or political assassinations provide opportunities, as do holidays. And then there are the ubiquitous animal or pet stories. There's one every day.

Most important to any fake story is a plausible, realistic edge with a satirical twist that is topical. I want people to be amused or amazed but fooled. I want them to say, "Unbelievable!" but believe it. Satire and believability are irresistible to the news media. Sensationalism gets them every time.

Q. Sensationalism is something that people regularly accuse some journalists of. What must be alluring about your hoaxes is that you present journalists with a sensational story. That is, they don't need to cover the cathouse for dogs or the cockroach vitamin pill in sensational ways. They're already sensational. Your hoaxes allow them to be thoughtful, objective journalists while covering something that's completely outrageous.

A. I'm willing to play the buffoon or the wacko and let them laugh at my expense, knowing I'll have the last laugh.

Q. How did you get started doing this?

A. I loved painting and sculpting, but realized how difficult it was for a young artist to be taken seriously by the art establishment. Also, I was impatient. So I began doing confrontational, iconoclastic performances, bringing my artwork into the public arena, like the Easter Sunday Crucifixion in 1966, which started when I dragged a two-hundred-pound, ten-foot-tall sculpture depicting a decayed figure on a cross into Tompkins Square Park on the Lower East Side.

These were the early stages of using the news media as an integral part of my work. These performances usually ended up badly for me and anyone associated with me. They were not humorous. I was scorned, chased, and arrested. But I learned firsthand how the news media operates by watching how they interpreted, changed, and misrepresented my intentions.

Q. How did the news media report on those early projects?

A. As a news story, I'm just a subject, not a person. My early performances were provocative, so I was stereotypically portrayed as a countercultural figure by the mainstream media. Not much has changed.

Q. Then the media became much more integral to your work.

A. I began to experiment, using the media as my medium rather than just a vehicle to report on my performances. I learned more complex ways to manipulate the manipulators, to bring attention to issues about which I felt passionate. My performances became, rather than simple political or social statements, more sophisticated theatrical productions, like the Vietnamese Nativity in 1968, where I constructed a life-sized Vietnamese village in Central Park on Christmas Day and had actors representing American soldiers with weapons attack and destroy it.

I combined advertising art and public relations techniques with theater, filmmaking, set design, research, writing, character development, acting, photography, and, of course, sculpting and painting. And I added hoaxing to my repertoire, where I would fool the media into believing total fabrications. I called these my "plausible but nonexistent realities." I was inspired by the need to be cunning enough to fool intelligent journalists, while leaving clues and challenging them to catch me. I'd given up the control a painter might have, but I was dealing with issues, with irony, and with worldwide media attention. It was no longer necessary to have a gallery in order to be seen.

Q. You've written that when reality as reported on the news gets as strange as it sometimes is, "pranks are needed more than ever to jolt us into reexamining our values." What values and what sort of reexamination do you have in mind?

A. The issues of my performances vary, but most of the questions buried in the work remain the same: What do we believe? Why do we believe it? This is true whether we're talking about questioning the authority of the media or questioning deeper personal beliefs, such as political, religious, moral, or ethical concerns.

My challenge as a satirical artist is how to present ideas to people to enable them to question and reexamine their beliefs. My hope is that my work provokes people to look at things in a new way.

Q. What sort of reexamination do you have in mind for the Final Curtain?

A. The theme is life and death. It's about as heavy as you can get or as light as you can try to make it. Hopefully, the Final Curtain has inspired people to think about how they respond to the death of a loved one. I tried to create an inspirational framework around an absurd premise to jumpstart the process. As it turns out, the premise of a cemetery theme park mall with a time-share program for the deceased may not be that absurd after all. Many people thought it was a great idea.

Q. How reliant are the reporters who write about the Final Curtain on the press releases you feed them?

A. Most reporters who come to me get their stories directly from press releases. Very few do what one would consider to be their professional duty. I count on this to a degree.

If I'm successful in fooling a wire service, I don't really have to do anything else to promote the story, because the media will feed off of itself. They all assume the original author did his or her homework.

The Final Curtain Web site contained a lot of information including contacts for the staff. So even if a journalist considered the concept over-the-top, there were people to talk with to get verification. Some journalists did call, which allowed me to have fun elaborating on the concept in order to convince them. Most did not question the premise but would focus on getting clever material for their stories. They asked about the artists' submissions. So I made up answers I thought they'd like.

Q. What sort of questions did reporters ask you?

A. The questions were quite typical: Where did the idea come from? When and where will the first theme park open? Tell us about some of the artists and their concepts. Is there anyone famous? How much will it cost to be buried there?

Q. Did any reporter want to pry into the story a bit?

A. A few journalists dug deeper. Some had questions about the backers and potential investors. But I'd answer probing questions with "I'm sorry, but what you are asking is proprietary in nature and I'm not at liberty to disclose this information." Very few continued to pry after that.

Also, I could always try to manipulate the conversation and feed them other aspects I thought might interest them. I'd tell them we were being besieged by the public, that we were really filling important needs. I'd speak of economic development for the areas in which we planned to build. If it was a radio interview, I knew they wouldn't spend much time. If it was a print journalist I'd ad-lib as long as they wanted. But it was relatively easy to answer their questions and keep them engaged.

Q. Did any reporters contact you, ask a few questions, and then not run a story?

A. A journalist from the *Bergen County Record*, in New Jersey, called several times. Each time he called he tried to dig deeper. Finally, he called to say his editor was not satisfied with the information, and he needed more. I told him I could understand the editor's hesitancy since we had not yet broken ground on the first park. And since I couldn't tell him exactly where the first park would open, "for fear that the information would drive up prices of surrounding properties," I suggested he wait until we announced a groundbreaking. He sounded disappointed that his editor was holding him back, but agreed that maybe it was best he wait.

His calls were particularly challenging. The Final Curtain office was not far from his office. I feared he'd take a short trip to our headquarters only to find it was a private home. But he never brought up the subject of visiting us and he never wrote the story.

Q. Before you revealed the hoax, the *Boston Herald*, *Mother Jones*, National Public Radio, and many others reported on the Final Curtain. Have any of those organizations run retractions or stories explaining the hoax?

A. Disappointingly no. Yahoo Internet Life, *Mother Jones*, NPR, Fox TV, *Associated Press*, Flash News, and the *New York*

Daily News, etc.—none of them ran retractions. Only the *Boston Herald* ran a retraction, but it was a put-down. And they were joined by the *Boston Globe*, which hadn't fallen for it. But then, I'd hoaxed both repeatedly.

Follow-up stories by those who have been fooled are rare. When it does happen, it isn't necessarily an explanation, apology, or examination of the issues brought forth by the hoax. They don't want to give the story any more attention for fear of further embarrassment. They don't want the public to question their credibility as an investigative news source.

Q. So your hoaxes typically get more coverage than your subsequent revelation that they are hoaxes?

A. The news media mostly choose to focus on the aspects of the story that concern their having been fooled, not the issues brought forth in the hoax. So the follow-up story is usually an admission that they "among many other journalists" were fooled by a hoaxer. They try not to mention my name. And if they do, they usually put me down. Not that I expect them to praise me.

Q. You ever have any close calls with reporters almost discovering you hiding behind their story?

A. I'm sure—well, at least hopeful—that there have been suspicious journalists who, thinking the story was bogus, decided it wasn't worth their time to investigate and let it go. But my experience has shown me that most journalists don't want to screw up a good story with reality, and they will talk themselves out of questioning the story to death.

I remember the first time I fooled UPI, this was with my Cockroach Vitamin Cure Hoax. When asked by another journalist for a statement, a UPI senior editor said, "The information was correct at the time." I never forgot that. That comment was the excuse he used to justify their incompetence. Incidentally, I've fooled UPI numerous times since.

Q. Has the Final Curtain received any media attention since, as the UPI editor would have it, the information about it now appears to be incorrect?

A. Even though the site has an exposé announcement on the home page, it still receives thousands of hits from all over the world every day. And the servers those hits are coming from keep changing. For example, last week I started getting hits from Poland. So apparently, someone somewhere is writing about it.

Also, I'm still getting e-mails from people interested in financing or mounting their memorial, or offering planned giving opportunities. Obviously people don't read very carefully. If I removed the hoax disclaimer, the hoax would continue on. It would be an interesting test, and I'm tempted to do it.

Q. Your Celebrity Sperm Bank, a plausible but nonexistent reality circa 1976, has recently become a plausible, existent Web site that auctions the eggs of fashion models to the highest bidder. In "Writing American Fiction," Philip Roth wrote, "The American writer . . . has his hands full in trying to understand, describe, and then make credible much of American reality. It stupefies, it sickens, it infuriates, and finally it is even a kind of embarrassment to one's own meager imagination. The actuality is continually outdoing our talents, and the culture tosses up figures almost daily that are the envy of any novelist." As a satirist, do you ever feel you're in a high-stakes race against reality?

A. Sure, but it also reminds me not to get old or culturally stuck, and not to be disappointed when reality beats me to the punch. It's a wonderful challenge. Not just to keep up, but to guess ahead of the crowd.

Q. Do you consider yourself at all gullible?

A. It is the fool who thinks he cannot be fooled. I hook lots of journalists because of this attitude. Especially Europeans who say, "You couldn't get away with that here." I say, "Excuse me, but I have."

But I'm as susceptible as anyone else. At the same time, I'm highly skeptical. It would make life much easier if I could have total faith and not question everything all the time, but I can't do it and I won't do it.

Q. What would you do if a Joey Skaggs impersonator began making hoaxes in your name, in effect adding counterfeit hoaxes to your real body of fake work, in much the same way that van Gogh's oeuvre, say, is today swelled by a number of careful fakes?

A. Are you trying to create more trouble for me here? Actually, I thought a lot about continuing my work even after I'm dead. So I've been designing hoaxes that can be executed when I'm no longer alive. For example, hoaxes that my friends can drop in the mail. I actually can still continue working, and no one will be the wiser.

Q. So you might create a hoax that's never revealed, that forever remains a plausible but nonexistent reality? That would be a fitting memorial for you, to leave behind some complex, undisclosed puzzles, a bunch of hoaxes without any end.

A. It makes the thought of dying a little more amusing.

This War Never Happened

An Interview with Sandow Birk

Sandow Birk is a painter living in California whose work typically mixes places and people that are recognizably part of contemporary California with classical compositions borrowed, with a sure but light touch, from artists such as Delacroix and David. His exhibition, *In Smog and Thunder: Historical Works from the Great War of the Californias*, commemorated and memorialized a fictional war between northern and southern California in eighty-three paintings, ink drawings, diagrams, three-dimensional maps, model ships, and dioramas.

I interviewed Birk by e-mail in June 2001.

Q. In Smog and Thunder features two large canvases that depict the land war in San Francisco. The event's the same, but the depictions are strikingly different. What were you after in painting two pieces of the same event?

A. When I went about this project my first idea was to spoof the idea of history painting and its role in Western European art, and so I went about looking at various battle paintings from the past and reworking them. My intent was never to tell a coherent, believable story from start to finish, but rather to make paintings that recalled historical styles. It wasn't important that they look alike. After all, the event they depict is fictitious.

Q. Do you think of one as offering a more honest picture of the battle? *Memorial to the Battle of San Francisco* presents the battle as much more orderly. But in *The Battle of San Francisco*, all the mess and destruction of battle are apparent. Did you paint the *Memorial* as if it were done years after the fighting ended, imagining someone attempting to tidy up the history?

A. I did imagine that someone was doing the *Memorial* painting after the fact, someone with the point of view of glorious deeds. That's why the sky is so much more romantic, as if all the heavens are battling, as if the event is so grand that the entire universe is involved. It also has knights in armor and tanks and helicopters and many more different time periods involved, as if the whole of history were involved. It's more over-the-top than the other one.

Q. Did you consciously want to create southern California art and northern California art?

A. I never thought of the art as being southern or northern. It's all based on Western European traditions. As the project went along I wanted to create the sense of a real war museum, so I added the war posters, the drawings, the maps, the models, and the relics from the war. Things you'd find in a real museum, like the burned flag.

Q. In 1999, you brought together all this material. What was your plan for that full exhibition?

A. It was presented as an exhibition of an event that the audience was familiar with, as if it was really part of our history, like the Civil War. When you go to the museum at Gettysburg, the exhibits assume you've already heard of the Civil War and are somewhat familiar with who was fighting, how it started, and how it ended. The exhibits discuss one battle in that war, rather than explaining the whole thing. I wanted to get that feeling throughout the project: that details such as these needn't be laid out. It gives it a more realistic museum feel.

Q. I like that idea of the exhibition giving only part of the story and assuming the audience is knowledgeable about the rest. Was one of the ideas you were working with that museums routinely make these sorts of assumptions, for good or bad?

A. Exactly. But for good or bad? All communication has to make assumptions and so do museums; it's not something singular to institutions. For example, when you turn on Monday Night Football they don't start each game by explaining the rules or what's happening or what the sport of football is and how it came about. They assume you come to it with some common knowledge about the event you're about to watch. Just as we do in all interactions. When we speak to someone we assume they know certain things, speak our language.

When you go to other countries, you encounter a shared common history but from a different viewpoint, and that changes everything. For example, read about the American Revolution in British books. In Mexico City, I went to the Museum of the Wars with North America, which offers a whole different look at our common history, particularly the invasion of Mexico City. Each of these viewpoints assumes a common understanding of these events, meaning that the Mexican museum assumes that it is speaking to a Mexican audience that has a shared view of the Americas.

Q. In your paintings you nod to Géricault, David, Delacroix, among others. Are there specific sorts of history painting that you had in mind for the two works about the San Francisco battle?

A. Your question raises exactly the issues I was most concerned about in the entire project: What is history painting? Is it ever real or realistic? Does it ever portray events truly? Yes, I was looking at two specific paintings from the past for those two works—one of the Battle of Waterloo and one from a medieval painting—but I wouldn't say that one portrays battle more realistically. That's the weakness and, more important, the strength of painting: its freedom from reality. My intent was to spoof and question depictions of battle, depictions of heroics, romanticism, death, war, etc., and the paintings that strived to do so with sincerity.

Q. But at the same time your work makes it clear that you see history painting as something with a great deal of life and possibility in it still. That is, history painting isn't dead for you, and it's certainly not all distortion and romanticism. After all, why create history paintings of contemporary California?

A. I'm not creating history paintings of contemporary California. I'm creating spoofs of old history paintings. My paintings comment on and make criticisms of the history of art and society, among other things. I don't really think that history painting can be done seriously today without devolving into

kitsch. I'm not sure it's possible to paint serious history paintings without having your tongue in your cheek. I've never
tried. When I have painted actual events, such as President
Bush visiting Los Angeles after the riots, I did so as much to
talk about painting as Los Angeles. At no point did I do it for
the purpose of "recording" or "documenting" these events for
posterity. That was the intention of history painters.

Q. A lot of the effort of putting on *In Smog and Thunder* has
to do with how it looks in a museum. The exhibition never lets
on that this war never happened, and so everything from how
the signs read to what the audio tour reveals is complicit. I was
wondering if you'd say a bit about the work that went into
mounting the exhibition.

A. Nobody is more museum-maniacal than Americans. We
have museums in every town for something or other and we
have one of the shortest histories to celebrate in the world. It's
as if we're obsessed with creating a sense of history where there
is none. For example, when I was living in Rio de Janeiro they
celebrated the five hundredth anniversary of the city. Our entire country isn't even half that old; our fixation on the Founding Fathers and the Civil War is absurd in the context of the
world. I was recently in Lisbon and was walking down streets
more than a thousand years old, and here we have the perfectly
preserved boyhood home of Eisenhower. Is that necessary?
What can we possibly learn from that farmhouse?

Q. That Eisenhower lived in a farmhouse? A lot of it has to
do with just being in a place that's notable only because someone notable has been before, walking the same paths and stepping through the same door. In Don DeLillo's *White Noise*, two
pop culture professors go to observe a tourist attraction called

the "Most Photographed Barn in America." People travel from all over to see the barn that they've seen in hundreds of photographs already. They buy postcards of the barn while they're standing in front of the barn. People go to the Most Photographed Barn to photograph it some more. They photograph themselves in front of the barn while holding their postcards. Is this all part of the same phenomenon, treating things as sacred because someone says they're sacred?

A. When I walked down thousand-year-old streets in Lisbon, *no one cared.* People live in buildings six centuries old in London, and they don't stop and photograph themselves in front of the place, even though someone incredibly important slept there, or was born there, or some event occurred there. Older cultures are much less obsessed with finding meaning in places and with recording events that happen today. Watch the NBA championships and listen to how historic every moment is, how jerseys are retired when players quit. I'm sure people smarter than me have thought about this a lot more than I have, but it is particularly American, and it might be something that *makes* us American. We go to the stupid barn because we lack something more meaningful. Or perhaps because we want, more than other cultures, for things to mean something when they don't.

Q. The labels in the exhibition are often critical of the quality of the paintings, or just plain dismissive of the artists' abilities. What were you going for there?

A. A lot of stuff came from my looking into actual Civil War history. That whole world is pretty funny in its deadly seriousness and excruciating attention to detail, the high tone of the writing, the overzealousness of its fanatics. You see the same seriousness in art museums and critics. Once I came up with fictional artists for each painting, it was obvious I needed fictional critics. I liked using these conventions to comment on my work, which, frankly, deserves some of the criticisms I gave it.

Q. I couldn't help noticing that the Getty Center is the site of a long siege and comes in for quite a shelling. The North, at one point, maneuvers a catapult into place and lobs appliances at its walls. Are you extracting your revenge as an artist, or does the military strategist in you believe the building would be a crucial position in any land campaign?

A. Both. It would be a very good defense position geographically, placed as it is on a high hill overlooking a main freeway. Also, the architecture of the place itself is very fortress-like. As an artist, the inaccessibility of the place and its location as sort of a castle over the Westside (the more well-to-do side of Los Angeles) is worthy of attack. But I have nothing against the institution, it's a wonderful place, it's got great artworks, it's been supportive of me personally, but it still remains difficult to visit.

Q. As I was reading through the press coverage of the exhibition, I came across an article subtitled "Painter Sandow Birk depicts the hatred and jealousy that emanate southward from S.F." It will probably surprise nobody that this article emanated from a southern Californian publication. How did the press in the North and South cover the exhibition? Did they take sides?

A. The press coverage was amazingly positive throughout, from both the North and the South. Almost everyone wanted to know who won, which I hadn't expected. It's as if no one liked not having the story completed, they didn't want anything open-ended, when in fact there was no intention of this being a story; it's an art show, not a narrative.

Q. That's right, you never really come out and say who won the war. Why do you suppose people who spend an hour or two looking at a complicated series of fictions want to know which fictional side won?

A. Many people came to the project wanting to know how the war started, how it ended, who was who, and details like that, but my intention throughout was to leave much of this unresolved. People's need to have it all spelled out was initially surprising, but not so much now that I think about it. It's much more interesting to leave the beginning and ending unclear, implied, and to leave the discrepancies, the errors, the conflicting elements in the whole thing. There are hints that Tijuana becomes a major player in postwar California.

Q. Is it necessary for people to know what paintings you're alluding to in your work?

A. I don't think it's necessary at all. It's enough for anyone to look at the paintings and realize that, whether they know which specific painting I'm quoting or not, I am appropriating a style of antiquated Western painting. It's pretty obvious that my paintings are intended to look like old paintings. That's enough to start people thinking. Of course, when one does recognize specific paintings, it can add another layer to the work because there are often particular references and comments in a single painting.

Q. What do those who don't see Géricault or David see when they see your work?

A. Almost everyone is familiar enough with the trappings of the Western art tradition. Anyone can pick up that these paintings look like old paintings, but that they are of contemporary people, which is strange right off the bat. Everyone recognizes the tradition of the horseback portrait, for example, even if you're from China or the Middle East. Why are people from our times being painted this way? What does that mean? That's the jumping-off point for thinking about my work.

Q. You're pretty consistently speaking in one sort of voice through your form and quite another sort of voice through your content. That is, your forms say: This is history painting, a classical work of art. And the content says: This is taking place on streets that look pretty much like how they look right now, in a place very near to where you are now.

A. I want my paintings to raise questions about classical painting. What was classical painting? Did classical painting depict the truth? What are its conventions? How does it relate to painting today? I also want to raise some questions about our lives today. Things like: Are our actions heroic? What is heroism? Are events in our time related to historical events? Who leads whom? Why is the LAPD out of control? What is the role of painting in a city like Hollywood? What are the reasons behind the animosity between San Francisco and Los Angeles? I talk about contemporary social issues like water use, immigration, languages, urban sprawl, pollution, among other things. It seems like a lot, but I spend weeks or more on a painting, so it's normal that the thoughts going through my head in that time find their way into the artwork.

Q. So you're raising and dignifying contemporary issues by rendering them in the manner of history paintings. That's a textbook example of the mock-heroic, where the trivial gets treated as extraordinary. At the same time, you're undermining those classical compositions. That's more like a work of burlesque, where the high and mighty gets treated as low and not-so-mighty.

A. Exactly. I intend to undermine classical depictions at the same time I seek to elevate the mundane.

Q. A lot of satiric visual art relies on caricature and grotesque exaggeration. Your work features not very much caricature and no grotesque exaggeration. Is there a tradition for the sort of juxtapositions you're making of the form and content?

A. Perhaps someone like William Hogarth, although he used contemporary artistic styles to comment on his times. And wait a second, isn't elevating stereotypical animosities between Los Angeles and San Francisco a caricature and a grotesque exaggeration?

Q. You're right. Pay me no mind. You got some grotesquerie in there. What interests you about Hogarth?

A. Hogarth was one of the first artists to produce work for a "common man" audience. Before that, the historical audiences for art had been the Church, the aristocracy, the upper classes. Hogarth made work about the common man to be seen by the common man. Through his development of etching and mass reproduction of his work, he even made his work available to the common man. Hogarth used conventions of painting that already existed, twisted them a bit and added layers of symbolism. He was critical, satirical, and popular, as in "for the populace," all things that I admire.

Q. The War of the Californias is a contemporary war, yet it's also a war that's memorialized in painting. As I looked at the exhibition catalog, what struck me first was the anachronistic details—the galleons alongside the destroyers, the battles fought on horseback and Harley-Davidsons—but then I started to think what is truly anachronistic is that this is all being captured in paint.

A. It's anachronistic to paint history at all today. I often worry that it's anachronistic to paint at all, especially in Hollywood. Most of the work I'm drawing from is from pre-photography times, when the role of painting as a means of recording events was necessary. Maybe I'm nostalgic for a purpose to painting in general, I don't know. Maybe I want painting to matter in a town where it doesn't seem to matter much at all. It's tough being an artist here, morally.

Q. In a lot of satire there's a naïf, this person who just observes everything that goes on and relates it without affect. The naïf is usually removed from his normal, comfortable time and place and dropped into some wholly different milieu. So that you have Mark Twain's Connecticut Yankee dropped into King Arthur's Court. Or you have Jonathan Swift's Gulliver removed from eighteenth-century England and dropped into the land of Lilliput. I wonder if there's something similar going on in your work, if painting in this classical manner is a way for you to observe contemporary people as if from another time.

A. A lot of the critical writings of my work have pointed out that I tend to have an outsider's view of things. Maybe because I lived overseas, in Europe, then four years in Brazil, among other places. I feel as if I'm part of my culture. Los Angeles has so many different cultures, from one neighborhood to the next, but I feel part of it all.

Q. What sort of perspective does painting like a history painter give you on contemporary life?

A. I don't think painting like a classical painter gives me any kind of perspective; in fact, it's the opposite: I live and am part of contemporary life, and part of contemporary life includes the history of art itself. I live in my times, and my times let me paint this way, or my times let me include these quotations from the past. I see myself as an artist today, and part of the language I use is not only today's, but what came before.

Q. Before you started working on the war paintings you documented news stories in South Central Los Angeles, where you worked, and often, you documented them in the conventions of history painting. TV and photojournalism now take care of the lion's share of that sort of documentary work. Do you ever wish that painters retained their role as documenters of reality?

A. No, I don't. It's better that painting is free to do many more different things now, that representation isn't necessary. For one thing, it frees art to comment on TV and photojournalism. I do wish that artists had more of a role in society, more of a voice in general. The audience for art is so small that it's almost pathetic. If I have a show in a gallery in Los Angeles or New York, it would be successful if it got four hundred visitors in a six-week run. Four hundred viewers, when I put a year's worth of work into something. Then some guy calls me from *Surfing* magazine, and I do a one-off little joke illustration for an article they're running and forty thousand people will see the thing.

Q. What's next?

A. I've been visiting and painting every single state prison in California. There are thirty-three of them. The paintings are beautiful landscapes, with sunsets and forests and trees, meant to comment on the tradition of Western landscape painting, when California was seen as a wild and beautiful frontier, a place to go west and seek a fortune, an American Eden.

Q. Were some of those original Western landscape paintings exhibited or published in newspapers back East?

A. Absolutely. And they were exhibited to large crowds to fuel interest in the West. It's well known that the underlying intention of the government, which sponsored some of the trips, and of the artists, who painted and drew and photographed the exploration of the West, was the promotion of California as an American destination. This isn't a secret; it was intentional. One important purpose of early Western landscape painting was advertising.

Q. What else?

A. I'm making the fake video documentary to accompany the *War of the Californias*. We're doing an hour-long film on the war.

Q. A kind of Ken Burns production?

A. A total spoof of Ken Burns's style, his plodding, solemn pacing, his seriousness. Very much a spoof on his stuff. After that, I'm not sure. I'm pretty sick of the war stuff though. That was what was so good about the prison project; it was a new thought process, a new preoccupation. I'll get to work on something new. I have a lot of ideas.

Old Master, New Mimic

In August 1937, Abraham Bredius produced a masterpiece. Bredius, the foremost expert on Dutch painting, examined a picture for a lawyer who said he represented a young woman from a wealthy Dutch family that had fallen on hard times. Two days later, Bredius declared he'd discovered a painting by Johannes Vermeer: "This magnificent piece . . . has come to light—may the Lord be thanked—from the darkness where it has lain for many years, unsullied, exactly as it left the artist's studio." With a brief letter of authentication and, later, a scholarly article, Bredius transformed some paint and a roughly mounted rectangle of canvas into a national treasure.

But Bredius was wrong. *The Supper at Emmaus*, as the painting came to be known, was a forgery, and not a crafty one. It depicts Jesus after his resurrection, breaking bread with two disciples while a serving woman holding a pitcher stands to the side. The figures are lumpy and ill-formed, their clothes concealing what the forger couldn't render. The space behind Jesus is unadorned, whereas in Vermeer's finest work, maps, tapestries, and paintings hang from the walls, and individually rendered tiles—usually Delftware, a product of the painter's hometown—decorate the baseboards. Vermeer's windows are often ornate and thrown open to the day, with figures mirrored in the glass. Light reflects off a bowl's lip or the beads of a pearl necklace and glows from within his human subjects. In the forgery, just the corner of a window is visible, and the only light is drab.

The *Emmaus* wasn't a knockoff by a lesser-known seventeenth-century artist or a student of the master. Not more than a few weeks old when Bredius inspected it, the painting was the handiwork of Dutch artist Han van Meegeren. While still a student, van Meegeren won a prestigious national art prize, but the rewards for being the year's best young Dutch painter were modest. He turned to forgery for fast profits and out of frustration with his contemporaries, whose abstractions and experiments he thought pointless, decadent, and dull. By painting in the guise of more famous artists, he became a shameless success.

The story of van Meegeren has been told before, in several out-of-print biographies and scholarly works of art history. Frank Wynne, a London-based journalist and the English translator of Michel Houellebecq's *The Elementary Particles*, adds little to those accounts of the forger's fizzy rise and ignominious fall in his book *I Was Vermeer*, published in 2006, and he only cursorily considers the uncomfortable questions about the art world raised by a forger's achievements. What makes one painting—or one painter—more valuable than another? Are such determinations rational, or arbitrary and faddish?

Such questions are, to Wynne, best treated as brief pauses in a brisk page-turner. He has his story to tell.

Reading this easily digested, only occasionally thoughtful historical reenactment is rather like watching the actors at Colonial Williamsburg or the weekend warriors who band together to replay the Battle of Gettysburg. In a typical passage, Wynne describes a domestic argument between the painter and his wife when they were alone, in which her "sensuous lip" quivers. Van Meegeren and others speak in so many unsourced passages of dialogue that one wonders whether Wynne has purchased liveliness of plot and character at the expense of solid history. His eagerness to embellish what is already dramatic leads him to overreach, not unlike Bredius and his expert colleagues.

The Supper at Emmaus is larger than most works by Vermeer, about whom so little is known that one writer called him "the sphinx of Delft." Its subject matter bears only a glancing resemblance to his better-known, achingly detailed domestic scenes—the milkmaid with a pitcher, the noblewoman writing a letter, the woman standing before a window as daylight shines in upon her. Vermeer's oeuvre includes few religious subjects, but Bredius and other prominent critics had long supposed that the artist, who converted to Catholicism to marry his wife, painted other religious works now unknown to us.

Those critics further speculated that there must have been a transitional period between Vermeer's early canvases, which tend to be larger, more romantic, and clearly influenced by Caravaggio, and his smaller, more placid later works. With so few paintings credited to Vermeer—in Bredius's day there

were fifty; today there are only thirty-five, and even that number is thought to be padded with forgeries—the critics believed the paintings of his middle period were lost, casualties of
time and the neglect into which Vermeer's work fell for nearly
two centuries after his death.

Van Meegeren's success in passing off his *Emmaus*, for
which he received 520,000 guilders, or the equivalent today of
about $4.7 million, encouraged him to continue forging. He
rushed off six more Vermeers, including *The Last Supper*,
which fetched 1.6 million guilders, and three other religious
canvases, which sold for a combined 4.2 million guilders—
extraordinary sums of money for any artist, during any age, but
all the more jaw-dropping when set against the widespread
deprivation in Europe during World War II.

Van Meegeren's later forgeries piggybacked on his earlier
work. He copied himself, creating paintings that resembled his
own fakes more than original Vermeers. Critics dutifully called
attention to the striking way in which each latest discovery was
so much like *The Supper at Emmaus*. In all, van Meegeren is
known to have painted nine Vermeers, three canvases in the
style of Frans Hals, and a couple mimicking Pieter de Hooch.

Through a web of intermediaries, van Meegeren sold *Christ
with the Woman Taken in Adultery*, his sloppiest Vermeer by far,
to Hermann Göring for 1.65 million guilders and the return of
hundreds of Dutch old masters looted by the Nazis. After the
war, van Meegeren was arrested and imprisoned for treason—
for selling a national treasure to the enemy. Six weeks in prison
extracted his confession: he was Vermeer. Few people believed
him—nobody, after all, likes being fooled—until he forged one
last Vermeer while in custody. Convicted of lesser fraud

charges and sentenced to a year in prison, he died in 1947, before serving a day.

Van Meegeren's patrons were not rich, uninformed collectors, people with all the money in the world and no taste. They represented major museums, galleries, and private collections. Wynne speculates, correctly, that nationalism and wartime anxiety fueled the intense bidding for the fakes. As the world came undone, the least the Dutch could do was preserve their cultural heritage. To seal the deals, the forger relied on the art world's overly cozy network of buyers, critics, and museum curators. That world, like all small worlds, protects its own. After van Meegeren's deceptions were made plain, few people sought to press charges. Most didn't want to acknowledge publicly that they'd been duped. Others simply refused to accept the truth. One critic insisted van Meegeren was a boastful liar, and prided himself on having rescued the fakes from being destroyed, as Dutch law dictates.

Van Meegeren understood, as other forgers do, that authenticity can trump art. The proof, however spurious and cobbled-together, that a painting is by Vermeer (or any other name-brand artist) is at least as important as the quality of the work. It was enough for the forger to create a plausible resemblance to Vermeer. Van Meegeren's early forgeries crassly combined elements of authentic paintings, cut-and-paste style, into derivative pastiches. While van Meegeren became an accomplished mimic, he was never a great painter. But he didn't need to be, for a painting's market value derives not just from the quality of the individual canvas but largely from the reputation of its putative creator. Today the art world is not appreciably different. Wynne concludes with an object lesson: in 2004, a Las Vegas casino developer paid $30 million at auction for a Vermeer that is far from the artist's best—and one that not all experts agree is authentic.

Everyone wanted van Meegeren's forgeries to be masterpieces. The buyers and curators wanted desperately to acquire a Vermeer for their collections. The critics wanted, no less desperately, to claim responsibility for adding one more work to Vermeer's all-too-slim catalogue raisonné. And experts such as Bredius wanted to confirm their pet theories. Pride and self-regard colored judgment, and no one truly saw what they were looking at, because no one dared look closely.

The forger's story may be read as an enduring fable about the art world. Were Aesop alive, he might cast the tale with a wily crow and selfish foxes. One day, the crow set the foxes fighting for control of an apple. The apple, the crow swore, was unlike any other in the world, and the foxes chose to believe him. But the apple was really nothing special, and the crow, in the end, was found out and driven from the forest for its lies. But what of the foxes that desired blindly and wildly, and so were fooled? Should not they too learn a moral from such a story?

Mr. What

Clifford Irving was once a household name. On December 7, 1971, McGraw-Hill announced the imminent publication of *The Autobiography of Howard Hughes*, a book Irving had assembled from more than a hundred hours of interviews he conducted with the billionaire everyone had heard of but hardly anybody knew well. An American expatriate living on the Spanish island of Ibiza, Irving had written several thrillers and then published a biography of Elmyr de Hory, the prolific art forger who could nimbly imitate the styles of Picasso, Matisse, and Modigliani. Irving, it seemed, sent a copy of that book to Hughes and received in reply a letter scrawled on yellow legal paper. The tycoon was impressed. "I would hate to think what other biographers might have done to him," Hughes wrote, "but it seems to me that you have portrayed your man with great consideration and sympathy, when it would have been tempting to do otherwise." No fool, Irving sensed an opening and so wrote back, promising he could muster as much writerly sensitivity for a book about Hughes's own life. To Irving's surprise, Hughes accepted the offer.

No one interviewed Hughes. Few people even saw him. A writer at the *New York Times* said, "It is easier for a camel to go through the eye of a needle than for a poor reporter to enter into the kingdom of Howard." In fact, Hughes was so skittish about publicity that he had avoided all contact with the media since 1958, when he wrote *Fortune* to dissuade the magazine from investigating his empire and to complain that a recent issue had named J. Paul Getty the world's richest man when everyone knew Hughes was. The story goes that he once elected to lose between twenty and one hundred million dollars in order to avoid a perfunctory trip to court to sign one document.

Publishers, of course, were hungry to bring out Hughes's story. The billionaire was catnip to them, and his worldwide celebrity and complete seclusion offered the perfect ingredients for a blockbuster. Biography, like nature, abhors a vacuum. Some publishers capitalized on what was widely supposed to be the public's bottomless appetite for all things Hughes by releasing unauthorized biographies and thin tell-alls, which, while revelatory, didn't always have the firmest grasp on the truth. In 1969, *Esquire* printed grainy enlargements of a piece of 16-mm film showing nothing more exciting than a man, said to be Hughes, wearing a bathrobe and talking on the telephone. Later, they revealed the film was a prank. But a Hughes autobiography—the billionaire's story told by the man himself, in his own inimitable voice—that was publishing's holy grail, and McGraw-Hill had paid dearly for the treasure, offering the huge advance of $750,000, with *Life* magazine kicking in a then-record $250,000 for serial rights to the soon-to-be epic.

A day after the announcement, the Hughes Tool Company denied that the book was authentic and sought to stop its release. In for many pennies, McGraw-Hill and *Life* endured a pounding in the press over the next couple of months. Still, they stood by Irving. The Hughes organization was a vast octopus, they suggested, and Hughes himself conducted many of his dealings in secret, sometimes even concealing them from his closest associates. After all, Hughes himself had not issued any denial, had he? His silence was said to be telling.

On January 7, however, Hughes gave a rare press conference and denounced the book. Seven reporters, most chosen for their familiarity with Hughes from the period before he withdrew from public life, gathered in a Los Angeles hotel room. Hughes phoned in his appearance from atop the Britannia Beach Hotel, in the Bahamas, where he lived, and for almost three hours held forth on everything from airplane construction to fingernail clippers to his affinity for shoes made of imitation leather. Although Hughes flubbed four of the six test questions reporters posed in order to determine his authenticity, all nevertheless agreed that he was no impostor. His voice, when asked about Irving and the autobiography, was unmistakable:

I only wish I was still in the movie business, because I don't remember any script as wild or as stretching the imagination as this yarn has turned out to be. I'm not talking about the biography itself, because I haven't read it. I don't know what's in it. But this episode is so fantastic that it taxes your imagination to believe that a thing like this could happen. I don't know him [Irving]. I never saw him. I had never even heard of him until a matter of days ago, when this thing first came to my attention.

Irving and company tried to hold what ground still remained. Irving claimed the disembodied voice of Hughes was only a "damn good imitation of what he might have sounded like a few years ago, when he was healthy." On *60 Minutes*, Mike Wallace grilled the author, asking whether anyone had witnessed his many meetings with Hughes. Irving parried with an entertaining anecdote about the night that he and his trusted researcher, Richard Suskind, met Hughes, and the billionaire offered Suskind an organic prune. Now Irving recalled that Hughes reached into his pocket and pulled out a cellophane bag of the snacks, though Suskind insisted it was a paper bag—just the sort of niggling, ultimately meaningless detail that nonetheless gave the impression Irving was a man who cared deeply about even the finer points of the truth. Wallace admitted later that he believed Irving. "The technicians," Wallace said, "the camera people? They said, no, he's lying." Irving, it seemed, could only ever fool some of the people some of the time.

Within a few weeks, federal and state investigators, as well as bank officers in Geneva, where the book advance was deposited, unraveled the story. Irving; his wife, Edith, who signed the checks and posed, with wig and forged passport, as Helga Hughes; and Suskind had very nearly pulled off a stunning fraud. Their escapades and the resulting criminal indictments, which ranged from charges of conspiracy and larceny to mail fraud and possession of forged documents, created an even greater sensation than the original announcement of the erst-while autobiography. British journalists Stephen Fay, Lewis Chester, and Magnus Linklater, the authors of *Hoax*, an impartial account of the affair, write that Irving got more ink "in American newspapers than the Vietnam War or the impending presidential election." Though they are tireless investigative reporters, their account sometimes turns exhausting, as when the authors record for history that a reporter, upon hearing Irving admit that his wife posed as Helga, looked down at his shoes and noticed "they were covered with fluff from the new carpet he and his wife had bought the other day." *Time* meanwhile named Irving "Con Man of the Year" and put him on its cover with a portrait commissioned from de Hory. *60 Minutes*, in what could only have been a late-breaking attempt at saving face, nominated Irving "best actor of the year in a starring role." A porn movie called *Helga and Howard* played to packed houses on Forty-second Street, and Henry Kissinger joked to the Washington Press Club, "If any blonde shows up in my bank claiming to be Helga Kissinger, she's welcome." In New York, T-shirts emblazoned with Hughes's face and forged signature went on sale, as did buttons that read, "IS THIS A GENUINE HOWARD HUGHES BUTTON?"

The autobiography wouldn't have been nearly as convincing had Irving cobbled it together only from what little he knew for sure, drawing on old press clippings, a few earlier biographies, and, most important, an unpublished memoir about Hughes confidant Noah Dietrich. Irving cribbed liberally from that manuscript, ghostwritten by Jim Phelan, a freelance reporter fond of wearing a coonskin cap and bush jacket when pursuing stories, who ultimately helped investigators prove

Irving's work fraudulent. Phelan's manuscript was the closest thing Irving found to a firsthand account of what Hughes was like. It was the fertile garden in which he grew his forgery. Still, to write an autobiography that persuaded so many editors at McGraw-Hill and *Life*, Irving needed also to supply the seemingly mundane details out of which all lives, even a billionaire's, are made. His story about those organic prunes, a story Irving told often and included in the autobiography's introduction, is thus pitch-perfect, for it humanizes a man assumed to be a freak and an eccentric.

All three fakers pleaded guilty, and Irving went to prison for sixteen months. His wife, who was little more than a courier and check casher, served a two-month sentence in the United States and then fourteen more in a Swiss jail. Suskind, who worked really as Irving's co-author, sometimes playing the role of Hughes as they acted out their fictional interviews, got off with six months. Irving, of course, wrote his own account of the affair, a book called *The Hoax* that was republished to coincide with a 2006 film starring Richard Gere as the faker-in-chief.

Irving's book remains an entertaining, though ultimately frustrating, account that reads like a romanticized adventure starring the author and his friends. Even people close to Irving are typecast, as when he describes his then-wife as "the hurt wife who feared the other woman." And Irving often describes himself as, literally, a character in the movies. At a meeting before two hundred McGraw-Hill employees, when Irving was sure his number was up, he writes that he "felt as though I were walking onto a movie set." His wife later imagines she's being followed by figures "like spies from an Eric Ambler novel."

Everyone's imagination can turn a little pulpy under duress, but after the stress fades, shouldn't thoughtfulness reassert itself and reflection replace the pulp fiction dreamed by our simpler selves?

Not so *The Hoax*. When first published, in 1972, the book was called *Clifford Irving: What Really Happened—His Untold Story of the Hughes Affair*, a clumsy title that has the virtue of making clear the book's actual focus: what they did and how they did it, but never why. When Irving begins to plan the caper with Suskind, he worries, almost in passing, about tricking his editor. She was a friend; she'd edited his other books. Suskind points out that, as junior as she is, she won't personally make any decision about the Hughes book. The planning continues almost without pause. Here and throughout, the logistical nitty-gritty—everything from the particulars of airline travel to a slapstick scene with a hotel maid, some credulity-stretching derring-do at the Library of Congress, and how the two men disposed of the typewriter used to create the manuscript—douses every ethical qualm in a downpour of details. The legal consequences of Irving's actions come as a shock to him. It genuinely surprises him to learn anyone views his hoax as criminal.

I decided to e-mail Irving to ask why he undertook the Hughes hoax. He'd recently completed a new thriller and, in advance of the movie's premiere, created a Web site where he made available information about his other books, as well as the complete text of *The Autobiography of Howard Hughes*. "The whole event, start to finish, was an adventure and a challenge. *Adventure* is the key word," he wrote me. "Not every part of an adventure is fun, but on the whole it's a lot more life-affirming than sitting on your ass at a desk stringing words together." But still, the ambiguity of his motives hangs over *The Hoax*, from its epigraph, which quotes Jean Le Malchanceux—"You may look for motive in an act, but only after the act has been committed"—to its end, on the day the conspirators pled guilty.

Irving wrote back, "I keep saying that no one really knows why they do what they do, they just concoct convenient and self-justifying psychological explanations. You don't accept that, which is understandable, but that's what I believe, and you're stuck with it. Any further answer concerning motive would be faked by me."

He added that Malchanceux's words were, in reality, his own, the invented work of "a fictitious crusader monk that a group of Ibiza-based writers used . . . when they couldn't come up with an appropriate epigraph or source."

Irving's outright suspicion of motives too easily offered runs deep. "You can't tell the truth about what happened yesterday," he told me. "You can only tell what your psyche chooses to remember. Everything is fiction."

People can, it's true, justify themselves endlessly, but is all honest retrospective analysis therefore impossible? In Hughes's *Autobiography*, Irving promises to relate not only the facts of what the billionaire did, but to probe—and even demand to know—why he did it:

> I wanted more than facts and anecdotes: I wanted the man. "You ask some tough questions," he said, and after a while he began to call me "Mr. Why," because "Why?" on my part became a refrain, until I was almost as tired of hearing myself say it as he was.

If Irving's imaginary interrogation of his fictional Hughes got to be grueling, it does, in the end, bear fruit:

> In the course of the next weeks he opened up; but it was a hard, painful flowering. Think how hard it is for any man to speak and tap at the truths of his own experience with a blind man's cane; because in that world of self-revelation we are all equally blind, or else we lie and wear masks we've collected throughout the years—collected, tested and saved for such occasions. But he tried from the beginning to get it right, get it straight, without the benefit of mask or mummery. . . . He wasn't aiming to polish his words but to plumb his memory better; not so much to be analytically deep, but more to strike the mark as though he were an archer taking aim at a far target and not so sure his hand was steady or his sight good enough anymore to isolate it from the background. He was archer and target both; and that was why it hurt, more so when he struck the mark.

In addition, Irving manages to see other fakers, those fellow travelers in the artifice of dissembling, with clear eyes. In *F for Fake*, the 1974 film by Orson Welles, Irving appears as an expert on the forgeries of Elmyr de Hory and speculates freely about the artist's psychology. "He has developed a fiction about his life," Irving explains, "and to destroy that fiction would tear down the whole castle that he's built of his illusions. The illusion, for example, that he's not broken any law. The illusion that the world has always taken advantage of him."

As Irving speaks, his pet monkey darts from his shoulder, across the back of his chair and onto a nearby lamp. He continues, "If you put it to Elmyr that he had taken advantage of people, that he had cheated people, he'd be horrified."

Et tu, Irving? In 2000, when Irving granted Mike Wallace a second interview, his own illusory castle still stood. Although Irving has admitted to the facts of what happened, he insists on viewing the hoax as an adventure, not outright fraud. Linklater takes a dim view of the author as adventurer and playful hoaxer. "Fraud is not only illegal, it damages other people," he wrote me. "There are no harm-free hoaxes, and Irving trampled over his friends, lovers, and professional colleagues in the course of his so-called prank." Wallace, for his part, was more bemused than tough-talking, so he and Irving spoke as old friends reminiscing. "I was filled," Irving said, "with the success of my fairy tale." He would explain no more.

The Confidence Men

In 1914, around Christmas, a failed cattle rancher named Oscar Hartzell joined up with two con artists in Monmouth, Illinois, and began plying Midwesterners with an amazing story: ordinary Americans stood to inherit a share of Sir Francis Drake's millions if only they invested now and entrusted the three to manage their investment and represent their interests abroad. The Drake estate, as the tale unfolds in Richard Rayner's *Drake's Fortune: The Fabulous True Story of the World's Greatest Confidence Artist*, was believed for centuries to be tied up in a complex morass of British law and genealogy. Hartzell and his partners in con artistry toured the Midwest, stayed in the fanciest hotels, and met with potential investors, eventually winning their confidence and taking their money. "Con," of course, derives from "confidence," as well as an 1848 article in the *New York Herald*, which reported the arrest of William Thompson, a new breed of thief who approached strangers on Broadway, asking them, "Have you confidence in me to trust me with your watch until tomorrow?" Thompson took the watches volunteered to him, never to be seen again.

At first Hartzell and his team approached people whose surname happened to be Drake, for obvious reasons. When that pool dried up, they changed the story: the rightful inheritor, they would say, a Drake nobody had ever heard of, living in some town where nobody had ever been, was too poor to pay for the intricate maneuverings necessary to unlock what was, by law, his. So Smiths, Joneses, anybody with a few loose dollars became targets for the scam.

Hartzell and his partners placed articles about this wondrous investment opportunity in local newspapers, which were always happy to publish stories about plain folk just weeks away from recovering a fortune from the British government. Meanwhile, new investors listened, rapt, as the three explained how a misfiled will and the absence of a direct heir meant that ordinary Americans were the rightful inheritors of the millions amassed by the sixteenth-century sea captain who was equal parts explorer and pirate. There were castles and manors and untold acres of British countryside at stake. There were rooms full of gold in the Queen's castles, and the Queen, moreover, knew it wasn't hers. They produced copies of deeds with official British-looking seals, legal papers, genealogical charts, land surveys, and calculations of interest compounded over four centuries. According to another document, the three con artists were the official representatives of the rightful Drake. Only they could successfully navigate the legal particulars. The potential return was incalculable; the multipliers grew higher and higher—ten times the original investment, twenty, fifty, one hundred—as more investors came aboard.

For fourteen years Hartzell spun this simple story an astonishing number of ways, and he was very successful indeed, leading a high roller's life of lavish hotel suites, leisurely meals, and handmade suits. When he was arrested, finally, in 1933, and charged with the distinctly unglamorous crime of mail fraud, he freed himself on bail and was immediately able to start raising more money from those faithful to his cause. Senators, judges, anyone with any kind of authority received numerous impassioned letters from Hartzell's investors, begging the government to drop the charges. Despite the letter campaign (one even reached President Franklin Roosevelt's desk), a jury found Hartzell guilty, and a string of unsuccessful appeals eventually landed him in Iowa's Leavenworth prison in January 1935.

In Rayner's telling, Oscar Hartzell was a clever, inventive rogue, rhetorically nimble at manufacturing an endless number of reasons for delay—there were, naturally, many delays in the settlement of the Drake estate—and justifying requests, of course, for more money. Rayner, who previously wrote *The Blue Suit*, a memoir of his own youth, when he balanced his studies at Cambridge with a line in stealing rare books, writes that he both feared and admired Hartzell, believing he was "writing both a warning to [him]self and an incitement to riot." Elsewhere Rayner suggests that stories of con men like Hartzell might be more instructively read as cautionary fables, their lives the dark opposites of Dale Carnegie's and Tony Robbins's, their unbridled pursuit of happiness justifying their less legitimate roads to the American dream.

Is it fair, however, to call Hartzell, as Rayner does, "an American antihero" and "an emblem of romantic individual-

ism, and capitalism, gone astray"? In the era of Enron and
WorldCom, of inflated profits and shady accounting practices,
is Hartzell a sign not so much of capitalism gone astray as capitalism plain and simple? Speaking forcefully without demanding much in the way of reform, President George W.
Bush made clear in his speech to Wall Street on July 9, 2002,
where his real concerns lay: the confidence of investors. Financial markets, the president averred, rest on confidence. "The
American economy—our economy—is built on confidence,"
he said, ignoring that an economy might also be built on the
strength of a currency, a manufacturing base, sought-after
products, a system of government subsidies and tariffs, or anything less ephemeral than confidence. As the president went
on to use "confidence" six more times, the distance between
William Thompson winning the trust and watches of passers-
by and corporations fudging figures to render rosier their fiscal
years shrank considerably. The distinction between con man
and corporation seemed less one of illegitimate versus legitimate than of small-time versus big-time. Edgar Allan Poe
wondered if con men—he called them "diddlers," the preferred
term before Thompson started working Broadway—were any
different from financiers, concluding finally that what distinguished them were the scale of their ambitions and the scope
of their undertakings.

But authors writing about con artists tend to prefer defini-
tions of right and wrong less slippery than Poe's. Judging by a
number of recently published books, writers often treat con
artists with dismaying simplicity, as heartless villains lacking
morality or as lovable rogues whose antics, like those of a mis-
chievous dead uncle, can be enjoyed from the safe perspective

of many years past. Rayner describes Hartzell alternately as a villain and a real rascal, which is either extreme fairness or mere indecision. Simon Worrall, author of *The Poet and the Murderer: A True Story of Literary Crime and the Art of Forgery*, treats Mark Hofmann, a dealer in rare manuscripts and a counterfeiter of Americana, much less ambiguously. Hofmann, who forged a poem by Emily Dickinson (the poet of the book's title) and profitably sold it, was actually much more active (and more ingenious) as a counterfeiter of Mormon documents, but then, *The Church of Jesus Christ of Latter-day Saints and the Murderer* doesn't have quite the same ring to it.

Hofmann was raised Mormon but was agnostic, and, as a result, became deeply alienated from the church during his adolescence. When he served as a Mormon missionary in England, he forged letters and religious manuscripts in the hands of early Mormon leaders that called into question the very foundations of the church itself. The church, determined to prevent damning archival evidence from falling into the hands of its detractors (including a rival Mormon sect), dependably purchased every one of Hofmann's shocking "discoveries."

Regardless of Rayner's and Worrall's opinions of their subjects, their stories of these particular cons remain focused on the con artists themselves. While this narrative strategy offers a pleasing dramatic shape—the age-old rise followed by the equally age-old fall—it comes at the expense of the more complicated story of those who were duped and why. Rayner and Worrall occasionally attempt to address this issue, but their explanations are often homiletic—at the level of noting, Isn't the public gullible at times?—and their attention always returns to the individual at the heart of it all.

Yet Rayner himself admits that the Drake con had legs, out-living Hartzell and evolving into those contemporary e-mails claiming to be from beleaguered, mid-level government offi-cials in war-torn African countries: They have some money, millions usually, it's in the bank and it's rightfully theirs, only they can't get to it, but with a little of your money greasing the right bureaucratic wheels, we'll all be rich and live happily ever after. Given the con's enduring life, how is it possible to view Hartzell, merely one of its practitioners, as its center? Examin-ing the history of the Drake con reveals that the seemingly unique Hartzell, whom Rayner describes as "an extraordinary figure . . . with a vast steamship trunk full of silk shirts . . . and a smile that demanded trust," and later, in terms that border on the mythological, as "a son of the prairie, of the American heartland," was, perhaps, not so unique at all. One hastens to conclude that, had Hartzell not come along to ply the Drake scheme or some facsimile, then surely someone else would have.

A more profitable line of questioning concerns what cul-tural attitudes underpin and abet such cons, because they expose inherent, gaping contradictions in the American char-acter. There is, for example, our boundless optimism married to our blind ambition; our insatiable greed matched by our lack of rigorous business sense; our belief in hard work coexisting with our dream of never having to work again; our insistence on high returns despite our being too risk-averse to ever realize them. It is safe to say there would be no Hartzell without these contradictions. As one famous American con man, Joseph "Yellow Kid" Weil, succinctly put it, "They wanted something for nothing. I gave them nothing for something." There would be no Hartzell, that is, if many people didn't desire something for nothing, and didn't see themselves, moreover, as deserving of a pirate's treasure for a meager investment.

Seen in this light, the Drake con becomes no more the story of Oscar Hartzell than the Enron scandal is the story of Kenneth Lay. This is not to defend Enron's former chairman and CEO, but merely to suggest that a mob-like hunt for a scapegoat to drag before a grandstanding congressional committee leaves largely intact a system of attitudes that assists, if not wholly collaborates with, the people who betray our confidence and walk off with our watches.

This unsuspecting collaboration between the con artist and the conned is the subject of *Mysteries of the Snake Goddess: Art, Desire, and the Forging of History,* by Kenneth Lapatin. Much of what we know about Minoan civilization, Lapatin argues, is the result of a pattern of forgeries. His book tells of the Cretan forgers of Minoan artifacts, working at archaeological dig sites and elsewhere, and the archaeologists themselves, chiefly Sir Arthur Evans, all of them eagerly hitching the wagons of their careers to the collective discovery of this wondrous civilization.

Lapatin, an archaeologist and the president of the Boston Society of the Archaeological Institute of America, has examined many of the statues and artifacts recovered from the island of Crete and concluded that the popular understanding of Minos as a highly advanced culture, a sophisticated early society rivaling ancient Egypt and Mesopotamia, is the result of a self-feeding cycle of forgeries and their academic interpretations. When Evans supervised the digs, he saw what he wished to see there and then published his findings in parts. As Evans's articles appeared, the industrious fabricators of the artifacts, many of them working directly for Evans, read his work and designed "ancient" objects to suit his ideas. Evans theorized, and the forgers rendered the proof. Everyone was happy with this arrangement. As Lapatin explained in an interview with his publisher, "The forgers got paid good money, collectors got magnificent artifacts, and scholars got more material with which to explain the nature of an enigmatic ancient civilization—one that was widely praised, ironically, as being surprisingly 'modern.'"

One of the central figures in Lapatin's argument is a diminutive statue of a Minoan snake goddess made from ivory and gold. Just over six inches tall, this sculpture of a woman holding two snakes before her, as in an offering, was one of the most famous and valuable objects in Boston's Museum of Fine Arts. Curators believed it to be more than 3,500 years old, but Lapatin told the *Boston Globe*, "It is at least eighty-seven years old, and could be as much as ninety-eight years old." The fakery is in the details, and here Lapatin points to the statue's head, which does appear somewhat modern in its shape, as well as its "pouty face" and "deep-set eyes." In addition, the goddess wears clothing that conforms with ideas about Minoan civilization current in 1914, when the museum acquired the statue, but scholars have since proved those ideas wrong.

In *The Arts of Deception: Playing with Fraud in the Age of Barnum*, James W. Cook identifies another collaboration between con artist and conned, surveying popular entertainment in the nineteenth century. Cook focuses primarily on P.T. Barnum and concludes that for all of the original showman's bravura about fooling the public, whether in his touring shows or at his American Museum, formerly located on lower Broadway, the public also willingly, even gladly participated in their own deception. Barnum's most famous and outrageous exhibitions included the "Feejee Mermaid," a creature fashioned from a monkey's head glued to a fish's body, and "What Is It?"—a racially charged Civil War–era act in which an African American man dressed in a fur costume bounded about the stage like a wild ape and then, unexpectedly, became gentle and human. The audiences for such shows were not so much being fooled into believing in mermaids and missing links as they were delighted by the chance, for a modest monetary consideration, to wonder whether or not they were being fooled and, if so, how they could tell.

Just as the Drake's fortune con never seems to die, neither do the forms of entertainment Cook describes. In his epilogue, Cook sketches a brief argument for professional wrestling and *The Jerry Springer Show* as reinventions of Barnum's artful deception, insofar as both traffic in audience complicity and raise questions about real versus fake, orchestrated versus unrehearsed. Entertainment formerly available to Barnum's patrons on Broadway for a dime could be had, for a higher price, at the Second Stage Theater in New York, where Ricky Jay's one-man show *On the Stem* played in 2002.

Jay, author of *Jay's Journal of Anomalies: Conjurers, Cheats, Hustlers, Hoaxsters, Pranksters, Jokesters, Imposters, Pretenders, Side-Show Showmen, Armless Calligraphers, Mechanical Marvels, Popular Entertainments,* performs acts of mental concentration, runs trained fleas through circus stunts, cheats audience members in card games, and, as carnival barkers and late-night advertisers say, much, much more. As a panoramic picture of old Broadway scrolls behind him, Jay tells engaging stories of crooked entertainers and entertaining crooks, including William Thompson, the original con man. At the start of the second act Jay appears at the back of the theater and proceeds down the center aisle, hawking "Ricky Jay's Chocolates" at five dollars a pop, promising that they are made from the finest chocolate ever known and possess aphrodisiacal properties. In addition, the boxes, some of them, include prizes, a gold watch in one, a hundred-dollar bill in the other. As his supply of boxes dwindles, and it dwindles briskly, he increases the price to ten dollars, and, almost at once, demand for a candy that nobody has tasted increases commensurately. Has no one learned a single lesson from Thompson, Barnum, and Hartzell? Even after the savings and loan scandals of the 1980s and 1990s, even after Enron, the dupes are still queuing up, as ready and willing as ever to grant their confidence and part with their money, all for the dream of getting something—a gold watch, perhaps a hundred-dollar bill or a pirate's treasure—for nothing.

A Holocaust Fantasy

In 1995, Binjamin Wilkomirski published *Fragments*, a memoir of his experience as a child survivor of the Holocaust. A clarinetist and instrument-maker then living in Switzerland, Wilkomirski related his fractured memories of World War II in simple, mostly unaffected language. He saw his father gunned down in Riga's ghetto, hid out in a farmhouse in Krakow, and survived internment at two German concentration camps, fending off rats and wading through excrement. Once freed, he coped as well he could with postwar life in Switzerland, where hardly anybody allowed him to speak of his experiences. Wilkomirski was three years old when the war broke out, or perhaps four; it's difficult for him to say for sure, because he received a new name (Bruno Grosjean) and a new religion (Christianity) upon entering his new country as an orphan.

Fragments earned widespread critical admiration and a number of awards. The *Boston Globe* praised it for taking read-

ers "into the mind of a little boy." Writing for *The Nation*,
Jonathan Kozol wondered whether, in light of what he identified as the book's qualities (austere writing, moral importance,
and lack of artifice), "I even have the right to try to offer
praise."

Although the memoir never became a bestseller, it did make
Wilkomirski a prominent and revered figure in the survivor
community. He visited the United States to address confer-
ences about the Holocaust and the memories of children who
experience trauma, and went on a speaking tour to help raise
money for the U.S. Holocaust Museum. At such events,
Wilkomirski appeared on stage, often wearing a yarmulke, a
medallion in the shape of the Hebrew letters for "life," and a
scarf draped over his shoulders like a prayer shawl. He credited
the therapists who had helped him unlock his long-suppressed
memories and expounded on his theory that therapy married
to historical research can match even the most fragmented
memories to real events. A child's fuzzy memory of a Nazi uni-
form can, Wilkomirski reasoned, imply some association with
World War II. Further memories, slowly elicited, can suggest
connections to more specific events. He often played his clar-
inet for audiences. If someone read aloud from his book, he
wept openly.

Fragments reveals its story in small pieces. It reads as if
something whole was shattered, and then left that way. In the
first chapter, Wilkomirski writes that he decided to stay true to
his memories by allowing the "rubble field of isolated images
and events" to remain a "chaotic jumble, with very little
chronological fit." Vowing to "give up on the ordering logic of
grownups," he constructs a puzzle of images seen through a

child's mental fog, without details or historical context. When a "gray black monster with a round lid" arrives suddenly at a Polish farmhouse, the reader must think "tank."

Before the book was published, Wilkomirski's agent and publisher learned of inconsistencies between *Fragments* and the documentary record. Production halted while they undertook an investigation. In the end, they accepted Wilkomirski's account of a Swiss-imposed identity, a fantastic and byzantine explanation that involved officials switching his name with that of a Swiss-born Christian child and then refusing, even still, to own up to their deception.

In 1998, Daniel Ganzfried, a Swiss writer who published a novel about the Holocaust the same year that *Fragments* came out, publicly questioned the memoir's veracity. Other journalists soon concluded that Wilkomirski was not who he claimed to be. He was an orphan, yes, but he had been born in Switzerland in 1941, not in Latvia in 1939. He was not Jewish. And, most damning of all, he had never been to a concentration camp except as a tourist.

Blake Eskin and Stefan Maechler have both written about the mysterious Swiss musician, and their books cover similar ground but in different fashions. Eskin was the first American journalist to break the Wilkomirski story. His interest in the author of *Fragments* has its origins in genealogy: his mother's family, the Wilburs, trace their ancestors back to a family of Wilkomirskis living in Latvia. Eskin's book, *A Life in Pieces: The Making and Unmaking of Binjamin Wilkomirski*, mixes his personal search for European ancestors with Wilkomirski's rise and fall and includes tangents into the history of anti-Semitism in Switzerland, among other subjects. It was Eskin's mother who thought her family might be related to Binjamin. She corresponded with Wilkomirski, and they exchanged family stories. When she saw a photograph of him as an adult, she felt certain. "A typical Wilbur face," she declared. Later, the family met Wilkomirski on a visit he made to New York. Their few facts and sometimes hazy memories could never be perfectly aligned, though. "If only we had the whole picture," Eskin writes of their meeting, "we could see how it all fit together, or we would at least know we were working with two different puzzles." Wilkomirski himself suffers no doubt. In his mind, all the Wilkomirskis are connected somehow. "It's not so important to know which generation back you are related," he says. "The human feeling is at the end the only important thing in life."

Maechler is a Swiss historian who was hired by Wilkomirski's agent to conduct a second, fuller investigation after the book's public discrediting. The agent had represented a number of Jewish authors, shepherded many books about the war into print, and overseen the Anne Frank estate. Unearthing the truth about the author of *Fragments*, however belatedly, would help safeguard her reputation. Maechler was given access to all records and received the cooperation of all parties, including Wilkomirski and his family and friends. Maechler's capable and exhaustive, but occasionally exhausting, account, *The Wilkomirski Affair: A Study in Biographical Truth*, published with a complete text of the memoir, thus reads like a mystery novel crossed with the Warren Commission Report.

Why did *Fragments* take in so many readers and critics? The Holocaust as a subject renders critical faculties if not completely silent, then at the very least careful, timid, and polite.

Critics approach books about the Holocaust with soft gloves, gentle smiles, and downcast eyes—witness Kozol's diffidence over whether he had the "right" even to offer praise. To be sure, Holocaust books can't be reviewed the way other books are reviewed, for the simple reason that the Holocaust stands apart from other subjects, posed at an extreme of human understanding and experience. At the same time, the effect of this critical reticence shouldn't be overlooked. It led many of those who doubted the memoir's historical accuracy to keep their reservations to themselves.

In addition, *Fragments* is a story that many people, guilty of nothing worse than being optimistic and hopeful, wanted very much to believe. The book promises that a young child, all alone in the world, could survive the Holocaust and live to tell what happened. Though the events it describes are harrowing, the memoir delivers comfort.

Fragments is, however, hardly alone in its expert delivery of hair-raising adventures eased always by comforting bromides. In 2008, Misha Defonseca, the author of another Holocaust memoir, confessed to fictionalizing, if not inventing outright, her childhood. *Misha: Memoire of the Holocaust Years* tells the story of a Jewish girl of six who spends four years during World War II wandering Forrest Gump–like across Europe, searching for her parents. On her own and by her lonesome, little Misha travels through Germany and Poland. She bumbles into the Warsaw Ghetto, she witnesses history, and she escapes. She makes her way through Ukraine and Yugoslavia. She crosses the Adriatic Sea on a boat and even climbs the Alps, passing through France before returning home to Belgium. Along her epic journey, she kills a Nazi soldier (out of self-defense, naturally) and spends two winters in the company and care of a pack of kindhearted wolves. The memoir, published in 1997, was translated into eighteen languages and became the basis for a French movie, called, in English, *Surviving with the Wolves*.

Defonseca is not, it turns out, Jewish. She was baptized in a Catholic church and spent the war in Belgium, with her family. When German soldiers arrested and later executed her parents for aiding the resistance, Misha's grandfather and uncle adopted her. Wolves did not play a role in her upbringing. Asked to explain herself, the author said, "Ever since I can remember, I felt Jewish." She added, "There are times when I find it difficult to differentiate between reality and my inner world. The story in the book is mine. It is not the actual reality—it was my reality, my way of surviving."

Books like *Fragments* and *Misha* are ultimately works of sentimental melodrama. At one point, a German woman promises young Binjamin that he will soon be playing and having fun, and then dispatches him to his first concentration camp, Majdanek. The narrator concludes, and the chapter ends, with the stunningly obvious and, sorry, cloyingly poignant line, "Majdanek is no playground." Elsewhere, a German guard kicks a wooden ball back and forth with several children in the camp. Binjamin lets his defenses down and, in spite of himself, begins to feel something like joy. "Then," Wilkomirski writes, "I see the huge, thick arm lifting itself even higher in the air with the ball, I see the arm swung back, I see bull-neck's face suddenly grimace, then I see the arm come hurtling down in a huge swing." The guard strikes a child with the heavy ball, and the child dies. Later, Binjamin sees a woman on top of a pile of bodies. She seems to be pregnant, and it looks as if the baby is alive, still kicking, inside her. When the boy draws near, hoping against hope, he discovers a bellyful of rats.

Such scenes, like many in *Fragments*, unfold with the calm-precedes-shock pattern that has become a staple of horror movies. Works of melodrama succeed because they go down easily, rendering what is impossible to swallow more palatable, flattening complex experiences into a series of recognizable emotional highs (those disarming calms) and lows (the jolting shocks), and washing it all down with a lachrymose moral: life for the children of the camps was no playground.

The real Wilkomirski's life, as revealed not in the pages of his own memoir but through the investigations of Eskin and especially Maechler, was probably no playground either. His living situation was sometimes chaotic, and his relations with others were fraught with tension and distrust. That said, having to endure a hot-tempered, depressive foster mother is not, by any stretch, Auschwitz.

Which raises an ultimately unanswerable question: why would an author take genuine memories of the farmhouse he lived in with a moody foster mother and set them several years earlier in war-torn Krakow? Fiction writers, of course, do this sort of thing all the time, but when Wilkomirski packed up his Swiss memories, shipped them across the border, and moved the farmhouse and all its inhabitants, he called the result autobiography.

When asked for an explanation or corroborating evidence, Wilkomirski stacks his fragmented memories of a war he never saw and pain he did not experience against rigorous historical accounts, and judges his memories more accurate. Wilkomirski seems less like a con artist, someone who has set out to deceive others, than like a man who has done a good job of deceiving himself. He has, to date, admitted nothing. The most he has said is that he doesn't care whether readers think his memoir is true or not. One has the distinct impression that he will always have his memories.

Lie, Memory

In 1973, at the Howard County Public Library, in Columbia, Maryland, Michael Chabon—a boy of ten, a Sherlock
Holmes fan, and already a budding writer—chanced upon a
book that not only fascinated him, but also, he said, introduced
him to "the first real writer I ever knew." The title of that book
was *Strangely Enough!*, a collection of brief accounts of supernatural occurrences, ghosts, haunted houses, and a flying
saucer spotted by a man in Yonkers—plenty, in other words, to
give young readers a shiver and some sense of a more dangerous, puzzling, even inexplicable world outside their homes.
Chabon was pleased to learn from the librarian that the book's
author, C.B. Colby, was a local writer, and excited to discover
that he lived down the road from Chabon's family, in "the small
cubistic house stained dark blue, with the goldfish pond, that
you had to pass whenever you went to our street's communal
mailbox." He decided to follow Colby, watch him, and perhaps

meet the man behind such tall tales as "The Bewitched Cat of the Catskills" and "Real-Life Jonah."

Chabon related this story during a lecture I heard delivered twice—in Fairfax, Virginia, and in Washington, D.C.—in May 2004. Brought to speak by Nextbook, an organization that encourages interest in Jewish books and authors through partnerships with public libraries, Chabon was the headliner of the season, which also included Grace Paley and *Bee Season* author Myla Goldberg. As Nextbook's public programs director explained to me in a later phone interview, "There is a writers' series where we bring distinguished literary writers to town to give a talk on their work in some connection to Jewish history, culture, ideas." Brett Rodgers, a fellow at Nextbook who introduced Chabon at both lectures I attended and moderated the question-and-answer sessions that followed, told me that Chabon "nails something that Nextbook prizes: he writes about Jewish culture and ideas through narrative." Chabon's lecture, titled "Golems I Have Known, or, Why My Elder Son's Middle Name Is Napoleon," describes, among other things, how and why he became a writer; how he came to write his first story (a pastiche of Arthur Conan Doyle, with a cameo by Captain Nemo); how he became fascinated with golems (mythical creatures made, it's said, from mud and clay, by dabblers in Kabbalistic magic); and how, over the years, he's wrestled with his Jewish identity and faith, sometimes neglecting them but more recently embracing them and seeing them as integral to his work as a writer.

The lecture is something of a balancing act and something of a smorgasbord, which isn't to say it's not engrossing. It's light and playful but also quite somber. Chabon has filled it to the bursting point with family anecdotes, and it covers more than thirty years of his life. In it, he tells stories of his boyhood curiosity (always getting him into trouble), as well as of his early experiments with literary style. Later, he describes his father's disconcerting habit of telling tall tales with a straight face; his parents' divorce; and, of course, the first and only time he met Colby, an author he esteemed who turned out to be a liar.

After watching Colby for several days, Chabon steeled himself and knocked on the author's door. Colby was kind but aloof, and recognized Chabon at once, calling him "my little shadow" and pronouncing the words with an Eastern European accent that reminded Chabon of one of his aunts by marriage. Like that aunt, Colby was a Holocaust survivor; and, like her, he had a faint greenish-black number tattooed on his forearm. Colby dismissed *Strangely Enough!*, his little shadow's new favorite book, as rubbish and told Chabon he was working on a memoir of his time in the camps. Colby said his real name was Joseph Adler; *Colby* was just a professional pseudonym. He indicated "the neatly stacked pages of a manuscript sitting beside his great steely battleship of an IBM Selectric" and told his young admirer, "That is the first book I will ever put my own name upon."

"I imagine," Chabon told his audiences in Fairfax and Washington, "there may be some of you who remember the name Joseph Adler. You may have read his memoir, *The Book of Hell*, which I still see from time to time in used bookstores, its black jacket tattered or missing." The book ("well written" and "fairly brutal," Chabon pronounced it) describes Adler's two years at Theresienstadt, or Terezín, in Czechoslovakia.

Chabon said he wondered whether audience members who lived in the area around that time recalled "the scandal that followed the book's publication." Adler, it seemed, was not who he said he was. A woman who stumbled across *The Book of Hell* in a public library had recognized the man in the author photo as Victor Fischer, the Nazi journalist who eventually succeeded "the notorious propagandist Julius Streicher." Streicher had been one of Hitler's early followers and the editor and publisher of *Der Stürmer*, a weekly newspaper filled with anti-Semitic slurs; both he and Fischer were responsible for having published glowing accounts of the living conditions in Nazi-run concentration camps. The *Washington Post* called Adler "the liar who got lost in his lie," the Wiesenthal Center had then taken an interest, and Adler, who at first vigorously denied the woman's charges, had eventually come forward with the truth. He was Fischer, and after the war he had wandered the Czech countryside, "penniless and starving." Chabon, in his lecture, says that after the war had ended Fischer was set upon "by a roving gang of Jews, bent on murderous revenge," but was saved "through the kind intercession of a Jewish girl, herself a survivor." Fischer—or Adler or Colby, call him what you will—then married her, and together they emigrated to the United States. Whenever required, Fischer had presented the passport and paperwork of a dead Jew named Joseph Adler, and on entering the New World he had assumed this new identity in full. *The Book of Hell* had been but the last, most dramatic act in his lifelong deception, an attempt to imagine a fake past to complement his fake papers. His wife aided and abetted him throughout his charade. Her "numerical tattoo had served as the model," Chabon said, "for the one which she herself had pricked into his arm with a sewing needle."

In a July 2004 phone interview, Chabon said that he's noticed audience members nodding their heads as he reveals Adler's deception: they recognize the story; they've heard it before, they think. Chabon's mention of Adler's homemade tattoo, at the lectures I attended, drew gasps from the audiences. In Fairfax, a woman seated a couple of rows in front of me turned to her friend and said, "That's sick." The lecture, which had bounded from light episode of childhood mischief to light episode of childhood curiosity, getting laughs throughout, had turned serious. The audience was rapt. The only problem was the personal story Chabon was telling, while he may have presented it as an authentic portrait of the artist, just wasn't true. There was no Adler, and no Fischer either, for that matter. Nor does there exist a Holocaust memoir called *The Book of Hell*, nor an investigation by the *Washington Post*. There *is* a young-adult book titled *Strangely Enough!*, which is pretty much as Chabon describes it; and it is written by a man named Colby—though he wasn't, it must be said, a Nazi journalist who disguised himself as a Jewish survivor and holed up in the Maryland suburbs. Rather, Colby was a real author, based in New York City and residing in Westchester County, who served in the U.S. Air Force Auxiliary after World War II.

For all his feverish invention, Chabon does make many broad claims about truth in "Golems I Have Known." Once, as he puts it, he "was afraid to tell the truth." Now, however, he's older, more established, and his Pulitzer Prize, which he received in 2001 for his novel *The Amazing Adventures of Kavalier and Clay*, fills him, he says, with "a sense, however mistaken, of authority." All these badges of stability have prompted him "to come forward now and come out with the truth." And Chabon's a careful teller of that truth. He delineates scrupulously—almost mincingly—those details he remembers, those he doesn't "remember all that much about," and those that are "hard . . . to remember." For instance, as he tries in the lecture to recollect how he made his way into his uncle's basement, an area off-limits to youngsters, he reflects on the distinctions between the truth he's delivering and the fiction he typically writes:

> If I were writing a short story, I would figure out how to get the parents out of the way, start them arguing bitterly about Vietnam or civil rights at the dinner table, and then have my fictionalized self slip away unnoticed, perhaps with a vague murmur about going to look at the money plants in the backyard, to head down the long dark stairway, into the basement, with its smell of iron filings and cold linoleum. Since this is a memoir, though, I will be truthful and say I don't know how I managed the trick.

Later in the lecture, just as the young Chabon is about to meet his idol Colby, the older, more established Chabon interjects to reflect on the ways in which his narrative—true to life, no matter how pedestrian—must regrettably disappoint any immature desire for drama or happy endings:

> It would be nice to tell you a story now about how Mr. Adler, the taciturn, intellectual, widowed author of two hundred popular pseudonymous books, and Michael Chabon, the awkward, unhappy budding boy-writer skulking around the margins of his neighborhood, his future, and his parents' divorce, forged an unlikely friendship while teaching each other valuable lessons about literature and life.

One can imagine here, without too much trouble, plenty of alternative futures for old Adler and young Chabon short of the "unlikely friendship" that Chabon broadly sketches, with all its Hollywood corniness. But that does not matter. Life, it seems, provided the young Chabon with no friendship whatsoever. "I guess that's why stories are so much better than life," Chabon says in his lecture. "Or rather, why stories make life so much better."

Chabon provides ample proof in "Golems I Have Known" of how stories can indeed make life better; but while his wordplay is nimble, the sentiment seems less noble in light of the trick at its heart. The parts of Chabon's lecture that aren't true demonstrate precisely how stories make life better by improving on it. They jazz up reality's details and significantly raise the stakes. In place of several actual and long-simmering domestic situations—a couple of divorces, a few arguments over religion—they supply the necessary tension and drama. In this sense, the lecture records a failure of the author's imagination as well as of his nerve.

Was the true story of Chabon's life somehow insufficient? I could see in his father's lying, for instance, a narrative about desperate attempts to impress a son and win him over—or, at the very least, crack through his adolescent sullenness. Perhaps "Golems I Have Known" is Chabon's attempt to take his real life and transform it into allegory, recasting it as but one chapter of the epic, never-ending story of fathers and their sons. While Chabon promised a real account, and suggested that it might disappoint our knee-jerk demands for drama, what he gave us instead was drama that diminished the life he'd promised to tell. Did Chabon believe that the reality-based memoir he presents in his semi-fictional lecture needed to be drawn more boldly and dramatically? "There's this very real sense," he told me, "given my family background, and given what I do for a living, where a fictional memoir is in many ways an accurate representation of at least a version of my life."

But isn't Chabon confusing his genres? Fiction relies on the audience willingly suspending its disbelief, casting aside their many doubts, however temporarily, as a demonstration of the faith they place in poetry, truth, and beauty. A memoir asks them only to believe, and listen, and experience a life second-hand. Chabon isn't just mixing fact and fiction, something all novelists do, going back at least as far as Daniel Defoe; he is creating a fictional memoir and presenting it as real.

After publishing *Kavalier and Clay*, Chabon received a letter from a fan who told him how much he had enjoyed reading about the lives of the artist and the writer behind the Escapist superhero comic books. The meeting of the Escapist's two creators came about when Joe Kavalier left Prague and his family in 1939, as Nazi persecution of Jews was on the rise, and escaped to Brooklyn, where he moved in with his American cousin Sam Clay. The two became friends and then partners, and the rest was comic-book history, at least according to the novel. Chabon's fan was writing not just to register his appreciation but to inquire as to where he might purchase original drawings by Kavalier. That Kavalier was a fictional character— and the book a novel—did not occur to the fan. Chabon related this story to me in our interview and later included it in a postscript to "Golems I Have Known," which was published in *Maps and Legends*, a collection of his nonfiction. On the one hand, Chabon said he felt gratified by the fan's interest, however naïve. Here was evidence that his fictional creations were being taken as real. He had succeeded. As a fiction writer he had received the highest compliment: his inventions resembled reality. On the other hand, though, he said he felt guilty for having fooled people.

Chabon's feelings about the lecture were similarly—i.e., confusingly—mixed when speaking with me about it. He seemed pleased to hear, for example, that his mother, when asked by friends about her son's appearances in the area, was able to keep his many fictions alive, even as she adroitly avoided telling a lie. "You'll have to talk to Michael," she told her friends. "I don't remember any of that. But there are a lot of things I don't remember." Chabon too does his best to maintain the illusion in the face of any questions. After his Fairfax lecture, I asked him about the Adler story, remarking that I'd never heard anything about it and expressing my hope to learn more. I was surprised to learn of a case of fakery as dramatic as Adler's, and didn't understand how it could have escaped my notice. Chabon said the story was hard to find out more about, since "Lexis doesn't go back that far." It was a line that he admitted, in our subsequent interview, to employing whenever anyone asked what other books Adler had written or where they could find more information.

When I initially contacted Chabon and asked to interview him, he declined, writing: "At the same time I have no interest in teasing out the remembered from the invented. It's close-up card-handling. I don't want to say how it was done." I wrote him back and described the origin of my interest in hoaxes, explaining how, in the 1990s, as a reporter at a business newspaper, I grew frustrated with the conservative politics of its publisher and the almost genetic lack of curiosity among the staff, and so began to write satiric letters to the editor under a variety of pseudonyms. As a result of that personal history, I approached Chabon's lecture—and his fakery—with sympathy, myself an erstwhile practitioner of the not-always-completely-true.

Yet I wasn't sure how Chabon fit into a gallery of con men, satirists, hoaxers, fakers, and counterfeiters. He was not like Stephen Glass, who had faked articles for the *New Republic*, aping the magazine's few forms—the profile, the hit piece, the policy argument—in order to get ahead. Nor was he like Binjamin Wilkomirski, exactly, whose *Fragments* was perhaps the best-known fraudulent memoir of the Holocaust. Wilkomirski was a depressed and perhaps delusional man who sought to explain the sadness he felt over his childhood—first orphaned and then adopted by a somewhat strict foster family—by finding in the Holocaust a grand sadness and epic tragedy he could make his own, declaring himself a survivor and then writing a fictional memoir about being a child in the concentration camps.

Perhaps "Chabon," the character in his lecture, was the epigone to Nathan Zuckerman, Philip Roth's fictional alter ego. Each sought to understand how experience mixed with imagination to create art. Each watched as personal lives and relationships were neglected in the pursuit of art, which always demanded more attention from its creators. And each realized the Holocaust provided a moral beard for a writer to disguise himself behind, silencing critics and their nettlesome questions. But *The Ghost Writer* was a novel. Not only was it clearly identified as such, but it also represented an occasion for Roth to puzzle over, wrestle with, and dramatize complicated ideas through his proxy. Chabon, in contrast, not only was presenting ideas as facts to a live, less-than-critical audience, but he was either blind to the implications of this or had chosen to ignore them. In truth, I would learn, Chabon was up to something different.

Chabon agreed to talk to me. With notions of magicians and sleight of hand never far from our conversation, I asked what the trick was to his lecture. Was it the way Chabon created something that seemed true out of a tissue of fiction and biographical fact? "There's such a long-standing connection between the idea of the con and the confidence man and the storyteller or the writer," he replied. But wasn't the trick on the audience, then, for believing what they were asked to believe by a lecturer—and expected to believe by a memoirist? And was it not a mark of the success of his creation that so many people bought it? Said Chabon: "I'm definitely uncomfortable with the idea of coming right out and saying, 'I just made this whole thing up and I'm passing it off as the truth,' which of course is what Joseph Adler did." I then asked if he thought that audiences have a reservoir of credulity for *any* story concerning the Holocaust, and if that means they'll more readily believe a story like his. He said, "The Holocaust itself, in its overall scope and its particulars, just defies credulity, which makes it somewhat fertile territory for deniers. Part of the reason you can just try to deny it is because it's so incredible, but it actually happened. But I think we expect the incredible from the Holocaust. The claims that I'm making about Joseph Adler and his identity theft are not that incredible."

•   •   •

The trick may be on everyone now. What scant media coverage there has been of Chabon's lecture—he's given it at least seven times—has not shown much skepticism, or even curiosity. For instance, the reporter who attended Chabon's Nextbook appearance in Seattle, in fall 2003, and wrote about it for *The Stranger*, the city's alternative weekly, dutifully passed along the story of Adler's fake memoir as if it were true. I wrote the reporter to say I was interested in *The Book of Hell* and asked if he could share any more details. He replied that he hadn't looked into it at all and wished me luck on my work.

Even Brett Rodgers, the Nextbook fellow, was no better at detecting fact from fiction, describing Chabon's lecture in an interview with me as a childhood story with some embellishments. When I asked what those embellishments were, he singled out the clearly fantastic: those golems Chabon says he has known. When I asked specifically about the veracity of the Adler episode, Rodgers said it sounded like a real story and reminded him of *Wonder Boys*, Chabon's second novel, in which the youthful narrator remembers an old writer who lived in the apartment above his. Rodgers added, "I assume it's real. . . . I hope it's true. If not, if he created a whole fictional identity, then he should be stopped." I told Rodgers the Adler episode was, in fact, entirely fabricated. He seemed shocked. "Really?" he asked. There's no *Book of Hell*, I said, no Joseph Adler or Victor Fischer. "Wow," Rodgers said. "It's not true. I'm surprised." As we kept talking, our conversation turned to other writing about the Holocaust, and what that subject required of authors: extraordinary care, namely, as well as accuracy of detail, moral seriousness, and an imagination tempered with responsibility. Rodgers said that, for him, Chabon's lecture did not raise any concerns. "He's not delivering a lecture," Rodgers said. "He's delivering a piece of personal writing. He's not making claims about history larger than his life."

Nextbook's public programs director, Matthew Brogan, who was responsible for arranging Chabon's lectures, described the talk as "both a kind of essay and a story at the same time." Brogan was by far the most skeptical, equivocal listener I encountered. "The whole talk plays with truth and fiction," he said. "There's a way in which you don't necessarily trust the narrator, and you feel that there's a way in which he is being both Michael Chabon and a narrator, and I think that's one of the nice things about the talk. . . . I definitely, listening to the talk, had a sense all the way through with all the stories that . . . this might be true, it might not be true, and that that's one of the things that you always are thinking about when you're reading or listening."

If there was a base, Brogan moved quickly to cover it. He would not be fooled; he didn't seem to believe anything very strongly, or else he believed everything somewhat loosely. Of the Adler episode, Brogan said, "I would not have been surprised if it turned out to be true, but I wouldn't necessarily be shocked that it didn't."

After the lecture in Washington had ended, several audience members mentioned the Adler story to Brogan. They weren't, however, raising questions about its veracity or eager to discuss how they'd been weighing facts against fiction while enjoying the talk; they merely wanted to register their appreciation, just to say it was such an amazing story. "My guess," Brogan said, "is most people assumed it was true."

Audience members I spoke to had similar reactions: They

doubted the golems—nobody's fools, they—but assumed
Adler's troubling deception to be factual. They just had never
heard the story before. A woman who called Chabon a "great
storyteller" said, "None of my parents and grandparents are
survivors of the Holocaust. So I don't really know much about
it from a firsthand basis. So I wasn't surprised that I hadn't
heard of it." Another woman explained away her lack of
knowledge about the Adler story by saying, "I'm twenty-three,
and I'm not from around here. I'm from Chicago."

On the morning after Chabon's Fairfax lecture, I checked
some facts. It took me just a few hours of digging on the Internet, referring to the Library of Congress and Books in Print,
and reading about Holocaust memoirs and hoaxes to convince
myself that I hadn't heard of Adler because he was not real.
Unless I'd remembered every detail wrong, I felt sure Chabon
had fabricated a Holocaust fraud. I was disappointed to learn
Adler's fraud had no basis in fact. I like such stories, enjoying
the many timeless similarities of cons, as well as the flourishes
and curlicues that set them apart. But I was also shocked
Chabon had put one over on his audience. I tried to separate
that shock, which smarted a bit, from my own sense that I too
had been duped. I hadn't nodded along as Chabon wove the
intricacies of Adler's deception into his own life, but still, I had
been fooled.

The story of Adler's fraudulent memoir is an intoxicating
blend of commonplaces about the Holocaust, survivors, and
their memoirs, with not a little sentimental consolation for
the audience. As Chabon would later tell me, the claims he
makes about Adler and his deceit are "not that incredible." But

besides being credible enough, the details are familiar, and what's more, they elicit familiar emotions—namely, a reflexive sentimentality.

"All the usual horrors are present," Chabon says of *The Book of Hell* in "Golems I Have Known," as if listeners know those horrors so well they need not bother to hear them again. He continues: "And although there is an interesting chapter on the secret camp newspaper . . . in the end there's nothing really to distinguish the book from any of the many literary memoirs that have been written about those times."

Been there, read that.

The Adler story, horrifying as it is, actually comforts listeners because of its details and its distinctly feel-good conclusion. Remember that Adler, though hardly sympathetic himself, is saved by a kindhearted girl, a Jew, at a time when so many others were, as Chabon's lecture has it, hunting through the countryside for fleeing Nazis. This girl alone does not exact revenge. But, by the story's end, Adler is caught; his lifelong lie unmasked, his deceiving days done. For all the derision Chabon heaps on his quaint, "unlikely friendship" with Adler, he too in the end comes around to the comfort of clichés. As in superhero comic books, crime, here, does not pay.

Throughout his lecture, Chabon celebrates the power of the imagination to do anything, go anywhere, create worlds, to fashion connections between disparate historical figures and authors. And yet, given the possibility to imagine the story of Joseph Adler, a Holocaust fraud, any way at all he wants, Chabon does so in the most obvious and ultimately soothing way—"Make it new enough" might be the motto here.

Of course it is hardly easy to write about the Holocaust.

Chabon told me he hesitates even to let it enter his fiction: "I think it's obvious from the way that I have treated the subject that I don't think I feel right about approaching it in any but the most indirect way." In *Kavalier and Clay*, Kavalier leaves Prague just after the Nuremberg Laws are passed. Settling in New York, he escapes the tragedy of the Holocaust. In "The Final Solution," a story by Chabon that first appeared in the *Paris Review* and was published as a stand-alone novella in 2004, a young German boy, orphaned and mute, takes refuge in England during World War II. Nobody in the story, not even the great detective Sherlock Holmes, who emerges from retirement to untangle one last mystery with a final solution, knows a thing about the horrors unfolding in Europe, and the mute, conveniently, can't tell what he's seen. The novella's title promises nothing less than the Holocaust, but by its very design "The Final Solution" blocks even the possibility of communicating anything directly about that horror. This is quite a tease, and a game of bait and switch on a rather grand scale. The structure of the novella also prevents any sort of adult complexity from intruding on the world Chabon has invented. His story stands between the complexity of the subject matter and the characters, holding the former back as it keeps his fictional people dumb. Everyone in "The Final Solution" is either unable to speak or ignorant, in the dark. This may be art made oblique by intention, but it may also be evidence of aesthetic timidity. The boy's pet parrot dumbly recites numbers in German, and the adults assume them to be some cryptic Nazi code, perhaps, or Swiss bank accounts—damned if they can make sense of the gibberish. The solution, though, is elementary, for numbers and the Holocaust do not together generate any mystery but rather represent certain blunt, inescapable facts, from the staggering number of the dead to the digits tattooed on the arms of prisoners and the chalk marks scratched on the sides of train cars headed for the camps.

In Chabon's lecture, Adler's Holocaust fraud serves less as a historical backdrop, or even as a story of the past told for its own value, than as a symbol to stand in for and magnify the personal pain Chabon feels: "Looking back, I find that my recollections of *The Book of Hell* business are mingled and effaced by concurrent memories of the Watergate scandal, and with the overarching scandal, from my point of view, of my parents' divorce." This is the Holocaust used, crudely, as a piece of heavy, somber narrative to drop in amid lighter fare; something to exert the weight—and gravity—necessary to stabilize the whole talk, the way ballast keeps a ship upright.

The Holocaust also deepens the dramatic seriousness of the life Chabon describes. It's his life, sure, but with the addition of a curious brush with the Holocaust, it gains in significance. That simple brush provides uncommon pathos. Chabon, like the version of himself he describes in his lecture, wasn't directly affected by the Holocaust. When I asked him whether he or his family had lost anyone, he said: "Nobody that I knew. Nobody that my parents knew. Nobody that my grandparents knew. None of their immediate relatives. They had all emigrated here." There was the one aunt by marriage, whom he refers to in the lecture, but, Chabon added: "That was the only sort of face-to-face person [who had survived a concentration camp] that I ever encountered until I was a grown-up." In fabricating his encounter with a fugitive Nazi in suburban Maryland, Chabon transforms an unremarkable adolescence, which still could be material enough for real art, into a broad fable about lies, writing, and being Jewish.

Faith, to Chabon, did not come easily, or without reservations. In the lecture, young Chabon is only vaguely intrigued when his father regales him with tales of how the family is related to Rabbi Loeb, the maker of the Golem of Prague, as well as a host of other famous Jews, including Harry Houdini, baseball player and sometime-spy Moe Berg, and Art Buchwald, the newspaper columnist. Years later, after Chabon decides to marry a woman who's not Jewish, he's less than pleased when his father comes to him before the wedding, drawing him aside at the rehearsal dinner, in order to reveal that he, Chabon, is a member of the Cohanim, the ancient caste of high priests. His father turns wistful as he says, "All those generations of Jews marrying Jews," suggesting, not very obliquely, that Chabon is disappointing not just him but now thousands of ancestors. Chabon's not convinced. Three years later, while living in Puget Sound, on an island—"I felt as if I was the only Jew living there," he says—Chabon and his wife talk about having children, but always end up fighting. Inevitably, he recalls what his father told him before their wedding. And he begins, to his surprise at first, to see himself as "the embodiment of a simple wish: let there be more of us, let us not disappear." The couple divorces. Later, Chabon meets the novelist Ayelet Waldman, "herself a product of Jews marrying Jews." They go to Jerusalem and visit Yad Vashem. "My heart was broken," Chabon tells the audience of their visit to the Holocaust memorial. "I came out into the sunshine and burst into tears and just stood there crying . . . that five-thousand-year burden of mothers and fathers and the wondrous, bitter story of their lives, almost knocked me down." Reader, he marries her.

In writing about his struggle to reconcile himself with Judaism, Chabon fashions a Jewish identity for himself that incorporates—through an utter fiction—the Holocaust. It's as if some encounter with the Holocaust—any at all—were a prerequisite for an authentic Jewish life; as if his life were lacking without it. In other words, he cranked up the volume. In Fairfax and Washington those amplified sounds played well to the seats at the back of the balcony, but they also distorted the minor melody underneath: those simpler, uninflected notes about a boy who wanted to be a writer, his family, the lies they told one another and themselves, and the boy's desire for a connection to something bigger than himself and his family and Columbia, Maryland.

Depicting those early years in a factually accurate manner has never been all that important to Chabon, though. "The whole idea of a memoir is a very dubious one to me," he said during our interview; memory, or the lack of it, according to Chabon, will always prevent any autobiography from being truly honest. A memoir, after all, is not all that the author remembers, set down in order, but rather what that author chooses to tell. As a result, all autobiography resorts to some degree of selective representation, which is but a euphemism for misrepresentation, regardless of whether it is made by choice or necessity. As far as Chabon is concerned, his audiences are there to be fooled. Readers of novels enter into a contract, he explained, which specifies that they're willing to be lied to. They want to be lied to, in fact. "I have no problem with hoodwinking the willing-to-be-hoodwinked," said Chabon, "or playing the game of fact-or-fiction, of creating a temporary sense of deep, vivid belief in the minds of people who know perfectly well that on some level it's all a sham." But his audiences at the lectures, how are they willing? They aren't readers of a novel, choosing a work of fiction with full knowledge of what they're getting. If anything, the Holocaust story and young Chabon's brush with evil make them predisposed to believe anything Chabon tells them. Chabon's ultimate concern, he said, was that the writing resemble reality. "It's . . . crucially important that it does sound true and feel true," he told me. "Especially feel true."

This emphasis on stories sounding and feeling true has a disarming simplicity. One wants it to be all that matters, even as one knows it can't be. Simplicity sours; at first attractive, it quickly turns naïve, as folksy as an unconvincing populist. In the lecture, after revealing that his father tells incredible stories about their family, stories linking them together in an elaborate ancestral web that includes even Napoleon and the emperor's nephew, Chabon says:

> I won't bother with the question of whether my father's telling the truth, or believes he's telling the truth, when he says such things. Nor is it germane to my point to ask if I believe him. After all, what he says could be true; if plausibility is good enough for me as a reader—and, hopefully, good enough for you as listeners—it's good enough for me as a son.

But is such plausibility, by itself, sufficient? In the lecture, Chabon trades away his veracity for it. It was indeed good enough for the audience and for the son, but the price seems steep.

In 1976, Jerzy Kosinski published a new, slightly expanded edition of his novel *The Painted Bird*, which presents a first-person, boy's-eye view of the Holocaust. Originally published in 1965, the book, Kosinski's novelistic debut, had courted controversy. Poles felt Kosinski had distorted their traditions and customs, making the motherland look tawdry and despicable. Anticommunists accused the author of going soft on the Soviets. Kosinski's mother, still living in Poland, was so harassed by investigative reporters and enraged citizens—few of whom had actually read the novel since the government refused to allow it to be printed—that she went into hiding. Some who did read the book assumed it to be a piece of autobiography dressed up in colorful myths and sought to crown Kosinski as the voice of all Holocaust survivors. Others suggested he had concealed from the public the truth, that he had in fact spent the war in relative safety. More vituperative attacks followed: Kosinski had blurred the truth of his wartime experience, inviting readers to confuse him with his narrator. The tale told by the "I" of his novel was not what Kosinski's own eyes had seen.

For the new edition of the novel, then, Kosinski added an afterword, an attempt, however fruitless and tardy, to answer all these charges. He also related his experiences after having published the novel, from the hate mail he received, to negative reviews and critical exposés, to a bizarre encounter with a pair of disgruntled readers (two men entered Kosinski's apartment in New York City intending to beat him with metal pipes—just punishment, they felt, for his literary crimes against Poland). But Kosinski's main defense was to declare himself a storyteller first and foremost and escape into the ether of his art:

> That I had survived was due solely to chance, and I had always been acutely aware that hundreds of thousands of other chil-

dren had been condemned. But although I felt strongly about that injustice, I did not perceive myself as a vendor of personal guilt and private reminiscences, nor as a chronicler of the disaster that befell my people and my generation, but purely as a storyteller.

He later justified his decision, which some critics called into question, to leave details about his biography out of the book as a way to focus attention on the writing, where Kosinski said it belonged: "Because I saw myself solely as a storyteller, the first edition of *The Painted Bird* carried only minimal information about me." As a storyteller, Kosinski didn't feel obliged to answer questions about his life, or to clear up any confusions (some of which, in fairness, he sowed himself) between the hard times of his narrator and the sweeter autobiographical facts.

Chabon, who has fashioned a memoir that includes not a little fiction, resorts to a similar defense. He turns dodgy about the fictionalized life he presents in his lecture, because for him fiction appears an almost lawless land, a place where responsibility does not extend and nitpicking questions about truth can be shrugged off with a simple response: *I make things up. I'm a fiction writer, a liar by trade.*

On the night after his Fairfax lecture, Chabon spoke again, in Washington. I decided to go once more, in part to check my memory of the specifics, but also to experience the lecture as a knowing listener, an audience member who knew he was watching a magic trick disguised as a memoir. It made for an amazing lesson in the art of audience manipulation. Chabon played his listeners expertly. The audience did not merely accept the talk at face value, treating it as truthful; nor were they merely entertained, enjoying a good old-fashioned yarn. They *believed*, and in believing they showed themselves to be susceptible to certain kinds of stories. But making up Joseph Adler and his fake memoir was not, it turned out, so brazen a fake. It was in fact all too easy. An audience glad—even eager—to be comforted got what it wanted. Except what it wanted, and what Chabon delivered, was not that inspired.

As I listened to Chabon tell the Adler story, I paid particular attention to his moments of high evasiveness. "To this day," Chabon said, "I'm not sure what became of Mr. Adler." Chabon's mother has told him she thinks she remembers that the old man died in a convalescent home; but she also, puzzlingly, recalls that Adler's accuser turned out to be mentally ill. What's more, Chabon's father offers an entirely different, even more baroque theory to explain the motives and means of Adler's literary impersonation. By the end of the tale, Chabon had so muddied the waters I wondered not what the truth was, but what his point was in even telling the story. As I mulled it over, my mind going in maddening circles, the lecture moved on, leaving Adler for Chabon's adulthood, and finishing up with a sweeping declaration, a grand wish for Chabon and his father and all of us to "be part of something ancient and honorable and enduring and greater than myself." And then Chabon added (coyly, I now saw): "And, naturally, I'm still telling lies." It was like the fine print at the bottom of a contract, a hastily inserted *caveat emptor* meant to absolve all the fact-stretching and outright fabrication.

Such elaborate contortions and deft escape acts, though intended to honor fiction, actually do a disservice to it. The act of telling or writing stories, in the final analysis, is not separate from life, true only to itself and answerable to no one. And readers do not entertain themselves with stories while resting upon clouds, perched at a safe remove from their grubby lives. No reader experiences fiction apart from life. Stories, whether written in a realistic mode or not, are in fact made from life. They are created out of it. And when life does not cooperate, writers make stories in spite of it. The substance of a story is the material of days transmuted by art, shaped by craft, and tooled by techniques, each a form of artifice and exquisite care that enhances fiction's lifelike qualities. No writer truly benefits from being judged by special, separate standards of storytelling. That's a recipe for certain irrelevance.

Liberties with the truth, so casually taken, also cheapen life, showing little respect or regard for the source of stories. The real life in Chabon's lecture, however much or little there may be, withers. His tricks reveal a crucial assumption, or maybe it's a telling anxiety: life is not enough; it is too pale and thin. Real life apparently requires exaggerated stakes—a few teaspoons of the Holocaust, say, or some other dramatic supplement to fortify the work's seriousness. What's worse, Chabon's trick defames the truth, treating Colby, a real man after all, as just so much handy material for a cardboard villain. In fact, Colby had served Briarcliff Manor, New York, where he lived, as a village trustee, a volunteer fireman, and the president of the library's board. Members of the U.S. Air Force Auxiliary, in which Colby also served, were civilians, some with past military experience, some without. They scouted the United States' borders in the aftermath of World War II, one small part of a frightened country's vast program to remain ready and vigilant against what was widely assumed at the time to be an imminent attack by the Soviets or one of their many Communist proxies. That story—about a children's-book author who patrols the skies, telling tales and securing the homeland—is, strangely enough, true and real. That story is not "so much better than life." It is life, and it seems a shame Chabon chose not to tell it instead.

My essay on Chabon's lecture was published in the April/May 2005 issue of *Bookforum* and generated a smattering of letters to the editor. The most vociferous objections came from Matthew Brogan, one of the organizers of the lecture and someone whom I had interviewed and quoted in the essay. Brogan posted his letter to Nextbook's Web site, submitted it to *Bookforum,* and circulated it to the media. On April 18, the *New York Times* weighed in with a 384-word article, called "Fiction, Hoax or Neither? A Literary Dust-Up," which managed somehow to be both nasty and confused. More thoughtful pieces appeared in the *Chronicle of Higher Education* and on the Web sites of *Inside Higher Ed* and *n+1.*

Brogan's argument was, in brief, that Chabon's lecture exhibited "all the hallmarks of a tall tale, with the author signaling to the audience at every turn that the narrator is not to be completely trusted." According to Brogan, I preferred to "ignore, minimize, or deliberately misread these signs in the hope of stirring up a scandal." Furthermore, I had dismissed "Chabon's repeated references to lying as 'the fine print at the bottom of a contract,'" Brogan said. "If anything, Chabon might be criticized for being too obvious in his winks and nods to the audience, but it is clear that he wanted them to share in the fun." Pointing to Daniel Defoe, whom I had mentioned, and Jonathan Swift, Brogan suggested that Chabon's lecture be better appreciated in the context of "fictions masquerading as memoirs." The authors of *A Journal of the Plague Year* and *Gulliver's Travels* "are not looking to put one over on the public for personal or political gain; they are simply employing a familiar literary trope, in which the story includes a fiction of its own origins." Brogan added, "Swift and Chabon make truth claims only to encourage us to question them."

Was Michael Chabon, as I argued, delivering a mostly autobiographical lecture about his formative years? A lecture that combined some clearly fantastic elements that were easy to spot (the golems he says he's known) with one central fiction that was impossible to detect (his brush with a Holocaust fraud)? Or was Chabon, as Brogan insisted, telling a tall tale and inventing for himself a more colorful and fictitious life because that's just what fiction writers do? When I spoke with Chabon, he never compared his lecture to tales like Paul Bunyan and Babe the blue ox or Mark Twain's "The Celebrated Jumping Frog of Calaveras County." He never mentioned tall tales at all. To the complete contrary, Chabon emphasized the sometimes painful, factual truth of what he'd written. The lecture explains how he came to be a writer and how he has wrestled but finally come to feel comfortable with his identity as a Jew. His aunt and uncle, he pointed out, are rendered so honestly that he thought it best to give them new names, thin fictional shields behind which they can still lead their otherwise private lives.

Yet for Brogan, distinctions between genres are tidy and as easy to discern as a red light from green. Chabon's references to golems were, he said, knowing winks that proved beyond any doubt that the lecture was not to be taken seriously as truth. Unfortunately, every other member of the audience whom I spoke with disagreed. When Chabon told them he once met a children's-book author named C.B. Colby, they figured he was telling the truth. When Chabon went on to explain that Colby—a real author, remember, a real man, not some character—was a pseudonym for Joseph Adler, a Holocaust survivor, they believed that as well. And when Chabon revealed that Adler's Holocaust memoir, *The Book of Hell*, turned out to be a fraud, and that Adler was really a Nazi named Victor Fischer who had disguised himself as a Jew, they were horrified and they were sickened, but they still believed. Why? Were these people all fools? Was each one tone-deaf and an inattentive listener besides? Perhaps not. They hadn't, after all, believed in golems, and they didn't miss Chabon's winks either. Rather, they trusted that a lecture might have clearly fantastic elements and yet still aspire to tell a truth. We many rubes included in our number Brett Rodgers, the Nextbook fellow who introduced Chabon and expressed surprise when I told him the author's brush with the Holocaust was made up. "I assume it's real," he had said to me. "If not, if he created a whole fictional identity, then he should be stopped."

I don't happen to believe Chabon should be stopped, but I thought what he did was worth writing about and discussing, and I hoped that the care and attention I brought to the subject more than made my intentions clear. Whatever we decide to call Chabon's lecture—magic trick, embellished memoir, or tall tale spiked with bits of truth—matters less than the nature of the trick itself. What interested me then, and does still, was how the intentionally distorted life that Chabon invented for Colby created a more authentically Jewish identity for himself. It's still Chabon's life, and it remains recognizable in its facts, but it's supplemented, beefed up, and made hugely dramatic by his fictional brush, as a child, with the Holocaust.

I could accept that Chabon's trick was part of what Brogan described as "a more contemporary exploration of the relationship between history and the imagination," if I saw any evidence at all that anyone had done any such exploring. Brogan told me he heard from several members of the audience after the lecture, and not one raised questions about its truth. Nor, he said, were they looking to discuss how skillfully Chabon had played upon their beliefs and levitated their many doubts. No, they just wanted to say how much they liked the story. "My guess," Brogan said, "is most people assumed it was true." Chabon muddied the truth of his life with his Holocaust tale, but provoked nobody to ask questions about this fiction in a life of facts. He appropriated the Holocaust for the gravity it exerts and then portrayed it in ways an audience would find comfortable and wholly familiar. That sounds like a failed exploration and, what's more, bad art.

Swift and Defoe did, it's true, embark on similar explorations. And they did disguise their fictions in factual clothing: a traveler's account of faraway lands, the recently discovered journal of a shipwrecked sailor, or a historical record of the Black Plague. But they did so with clear purpose and evident design. They didn't seek to comfort their readers. Nor did they imagine themselves as humble tellers of tall tales. Moreover, they often hid their fictions because they had little choice. Writing fiction was not considered a respectable occupation.

Novels were trash, largely, just crude entertainments. Had the term "literary novel" existed, it would have been an oxymoron. Swift and Defoe disguised their fictions for aesthetic reasons too. They wanted to raise questions more taxing—and more urgent—than *Is this real, or am I just making it all up?* They wanted to accomplish something more than merely invite their readers to "share in the fun."

Gulliver's Travels remains a piece of serious fun. The specifics of Swift's satire may be lost on all but the most specialized readers—who not armed with a Norton critical edition can suss out Swift's sentiments about religious tolerance in Holland or get the jokes he tells at Charles V's expense?—but what remains is a broader comedy, a satire on humankind, hypocrisy, selfishness and cruelty, egotism and the solipsism of intellectuals. That satire still makes great demands on the audience. It doesn't just entertain, nor does it baffle and fool. It asks readers to wonder at how inhumanely they, the dear readers, treat one another. It is unsparing, and it never lets a single reader off the hook. "Satire," Swift knew, "is a sort of glass, wherein beholders do generally discover everybody's face but their own." That's a pessimistic note for such an accomplished satirist to strike, but he wrote it, tellingly, at the beginning of another satire, *The Battle of the Books*. Swift was being hopeful; at least, as much as he ever was. He was trying again, once more, to reach out to readers and demand from them great intelligence and imagination and rigor. Writing, after all, needn't be a mirror in which authors discover only themselves looking back and grinning. Is it a cause for scandal, really, to expect as much from an author today?